–NESS.docs

2

Landscape as Urbanism
in the Americas

Lots of Architecture
– publishers

Over the past quarter century landscape has been claimed as model and medium for the contemporary city. During this time a range of alternative architectural and urban practices have emerged across Latin America. Many of these practices explore the ecological and territorial implications for the urban project.

—Charles Waldheim

Landscape as Urbanism in the Americas focuses on the potentials for landscape as a medium of urban intervention in the cultural, economic, and ecological contexts of Latin America.

During our first speculations about –NESS.docs, we had already decided that our monographic series would not only feature individual practices but also address topics that we thought deserved visibility, discussion, and reflection.

Another relevant fact is that, for a long time, we have devoted a good part of our careers to the promotion and reinforcement of the North-South/South-North network.

This issue puts together these intentions and presents a group of very interesting Latin American practices, while feeling like a very organic outcome of the spontaneous dialogues that started with Charles Waldheim and Luis Callejas around seven years ago in a very red and picturesque Cambridge fall. The conversation continued in different cities and formats as we accompanied and witnessed the development of the Landscape as Urbanism in the Americas initiative.

Latin America is a vivid territory, it is messy, exuberant, full of colors, sounds, music, and aromas. It is not at all a uniform continent, and it is not fair to think about it as a whole without fractures. The common ground resides in its colonial history and its later modernization phases, in the extraction of raw materials, and some complex political junctures during the last centuries. And there is the language too, of course. Also, some geographical entities and the ecosystems they generate are sometimes more definitory of certain idiosyncrasies and modes of inhabiting than the political borders.

In –NESS.docs 2, *Landscape as Urbanism in the Americas. Potentials for landscape as a medium for urban intervention in cultural, economic, and ecological contexts of Latin America*, there is a very conscious effort to take a critical distance from the usual readings of Latin American projects. We intended to force a degree of reflexive abstraction and encourage new understandings of these practices, posing them as part of a much wider scenario.

We have edited this publication with Mercedes Peralta and Jeannette Sordi. Both have been involved in different stages with the Office for Urbanization founded by Charles Waldheim, who has generously supported and overviewed the curatorial process. We are also very grateful to the Harvard University's David Rockefeller Center for Latin American Studies for helping to make this possible.

For Lots of Architecture, this is a new step in our pledge to explore and promote challenging dialogues.

Pablo Gerson &
Florencia Rodriguez

A New Language

CHARLES WALDHEIM

The discourse and practices of landscape urbanism emerged a quarter century ago in Western Europe and North America in relation to two distinct disciplinary shifts. A generation of architects concerned with the city yet critical of the dominant neoconservative and new urbanist practices of the day found in program and event surrogates for urbanity that, in lieu of the masterplan, opted for open-endedness, indeterminacy, and change over time. Simultaneously, a generation of landscape architects trained in regional ecological planning sought to revive their discipline through the curation of ecologies as media of design for the contemporary public realm. These two complementary conditions intersected in the mid-1990s to produce a new object, a new language. (1) While landscape urbanism emerged in a dialogue between architects and landscape architects working in the United States, the United Kingdom, and the Netherlands, it has gone on to form a global conversation. Over the past quarter century since the emergence of landscape urbanism, landscape has been reclaimed as a model and medium for the contemporary city. These practices, found in every corner of the world, have been fueled by neoliberal economic structures and the increasing demand for environmentally-informed and ecologically-minded urban design and planning. During this time, a range of alternative architectural and urban practices have emerged across Latin America, many of which explore the ecological and territorial implications for the urban project.

While there remain enormous cultural differences across the continent, Latin American architects have had a longstanding tradition of education abroad, and many Colombian, Argentinian, Chilean, and Mexican architects have historically traveled to Spain for architectural education and professional experience. In the 1990s, Latin American architects abroad witnessed the enormous impact of landscape projects in the renewal of Barcelona's public realm. During the 1990s and 2000s, many Latin American architects also went to the Netherlands and the United Kingdom, where they encountered the resurgent role of landscape in the discourse and practices of contemporary urbanism. More recently, Latin American architects studying in North America would have encountered the emergence of landscape urbanism. While some stayed to pursue their careers in Europe or the United States, many also returned to Latin America, where they found the professional, cultural, and political context for imagining large public works projects through the lens of landscape. In the years since the appearance of landscape urbanism in English-language discourse, many Latin American architects educated abroad have returned to roles of significance in professional practice, architectural education, and cultural production. These architects often evince in their work—across various media and modes of production—a renewed interest in ecological and biological models and metaphors. More recently, a number of individuals and institutions across Latin America have committed to the articulation of landscape architecture as a distinct disciplinary and professional identity. While the status and future

(1) "Interdisciplinarity is not the calm of an easy security; it begins effectively . . . when the solidarity of the old disciplines breaks down—perhaps even violently, via the jolts of fashion—in the interests of a new object and a new language." Barthes, Roland. From Work to Text, in "Image, Music, Text," translated by Stephen Heath, New York: Hill and Wang, 1977, p. 155.

of those efforts vary greatly from country to country and culture to culture, new academic programs and initiatives concerning landscape and landscape architecture can currently be found in many cities across the region.

Both of these tendencies—the ascendance of biological and ecological models for architectural thought and the interest in landscape architecture as a professional identity—have been enabled by social, economic, and political transformations. While we must acknowledge the great differences across the cultures and countries of the region where some (Brazil, for example) have long benefited from a tradition of landscape architecture, others (Colombia, Argentina, Chile, or Mexico, for example) have not. In either case, the general tendency toward democratization and neoliberal economic models in the region have fueled a political economy in which the public works programs of Latin American cities have increasingly enabled a generation of architects to imagine the renewal of the public realm through the medium of landscape. Their projects have been enabled by public expectations for the renewal of redundant uses and the enhancement of the environmental quality of the public realm.

The *Landscape as Urbanism in the Americas* initiative originated five years ago as an organic conversation amongst a range of Latin American architects, urbanists, and educators. The initiative convened a series of discussions on the potentials for landscape as a medium of urban intervention in the specific social, cultural, economic, and ecological contexts of Latin American cities. The traveling program of conferences that emerged from those conversations and this volume of –NESS.docs aspire to assemble a set of projects, practices, and potentials in the interests of forming a new language, one specifically deriving from the conditions and cultures of the Americas.

We remain indebted to all of our colleagues and contributors who have conspired to make this initiative possible. We are particularly grateful to Felipe Vera for first proposing such an initiative, to Marcela Ramos for supporting it materially and institutionally, to Luis Callejas and Jeannette Sordi for conceptualizing and mobilizing the idea, to Helen Kongsgaard and Pedro Aparicio for enabling its earliest manifestations, to Mercedes Peralta for imagining and managing its ultimate realization, and to Florencia Rodriguez and her team at –NESS for the making of this publication. The initiative would not have been possible without the generous support of the Harvard University Graduate School of Design, Harvard University's Rockefeller Center for Latin American Studies, as well as our partnering individuals, institutions, and organizations across the region.

Charles Waldheim *is a North American architect, urbanist, and educator. His research and practice examine the relations between landscape, ecology, and contemporary urbanism. He coined the term "landscape urbanism" to describe the emergent discourse and practices of landscape in relation to design culture and contemporary urbanization. On these topics, Waldheim is author of "Landscape as Urbanism: A General Theory" and editor of "The Landscape Urbanism Reader." Waldheim is John E. Irving Professor of Landscape Architecture at the Harvard University Graduate School of Design where he directs the School's Office for Urbanization.*

Landscape as Urbanism in Latin America

Environment, Ground, System, Protocol, Nature

MERCEDES PERALTA & JEANNETTE SORDI

This edition of –NESS.docs represents a new editorial and curatorial avenue for the *Landscape as Urbanism in the Americas* project, an initiative that has brought together almost one hundred professionals, scholars, and city leaders over the past five years. Until now, the project has been convened primarily as a series of conferences. These have been held in Medellín (2016), Santiago (2016), Brasilia (2016), Mexico City (2017), and Buenos Aires (2018), with the addition of an upcoming sixth conference that will take place at the Harvard University Graduate School of Design (GSD) in March 2020. In addition, the initiative's digital archive includes a collection of more than sixty featured landscape urbanist projects in Latin America. (1)

This multi-series project has been made possible through the collaboration of thirty-eight institutions. It has proceeded under the leadership of the GSD's Office for Urbanization and with the constant support of the Harvard University's David Rockefeller Center for Latin American Studies. (2) A truly collective endeavor, *Landscape as Urbanism in the Americas* has resulted in a multifaceted portrait of current discussions on landscape as urbanism across the Americas, becoming itself a medium for new dialogues, partnerships, and fields of inquiry.

The aim of –NESS.docs.02: *Landscape as Urbanism in the Americas* is to capture the scope of this initiative in order to critically sustain and foster exchange among an international community involved in the study of architecture, landscape, and urbanism. This endeavor demands a framework that can critically question and reposition projects thematically. The works included here reinterpret and complement the list of projects in the digital archive and are arranged as a constellation of ideas linked to current and potential future discussions around the discipline. By framing these projects around a set of five specific themes, we aim to interrogate topics such as the emerging social life arising from new economies, new kinds of collaboration between humans and other species, emerging approaches toward shared living spaces, nature and environmental transformation, inclusion and public space, and the need for intra-disciplinary design approaches in an age of ecological crisis.

The first theme, Biological Environments, features material and representational strategies that use biological metaphors as a point of departure for design. It includes the Jardín Botánico in Culiacán, México, by Tatiana Bilbao Estudio; Supertourism, a tourism proposal by Fábrica de Paisaje; Edificio Jardín Hospedero y Nectarífero para Mariposas by Husos; Pharma – Park, Landscape for Biochemical Ecology by Camilo Restrepo in Antioquia, Colombia; and CAPA's Multisensory Carpet.

(1) The project archive, along with programs and videos of the *Landscape as Urbanism in the Americas* events held in Medellín, Santiago, Brasilia, Mexico, and Buenos Aires, are available on the website of the initiative, landscapeasurbanismamericas.net.

(2) For a description of the initiative and a complete list of its participants please see p. 191. The Harvard GSD conference will be held on March 27-28, 2020.

Resilient Grounds brings together proposals foregrounding the social and political discourse of landscape urbanism, showing its capacity for relating to broader audiences through public works. Such projects include Paseo Cívico Metropolitano - Alameda Providencia Corridor by Groundlab, LyonBosch+Martic, Idom, and Sergio Chiquetto; Dom Pedro II Park by FUPAM / LUME, H+F Arquitetos, Metrópole Arquitetos, and UNA Arquitetos; Metro Arquitetos Associados' Ladeira da Barroquinha; Opera Publica's El Grito de Alcorta in Argentina, and Plaza Jorge Somaca by Enlace Arquitectura.

Performative Systems examines program-oriented approaches driven by ecological performance. It is comprised of the Aquatic Center by Luis Callejas (LCLA Office), Edgar Mazo, and Sebastián Mejía; Bulla's Parque del Centro de Exposiciones y Convenciones; Juan David Hoyos and Sebastián Monsalve's Parque Botánico Río Medellín; and RDR Architects' Plaza Houssay, a transformation of public space in Buenos Aires; and The Garden of Forking Paths, a site-specific installation by Beals Lyon Arquitectos.

Revealed Protocols collects systemic and diagrammatic procedures, highlighting formal schemes that aim for large-scale innovation. It includes LCLA Office's Pelagic Alphabet; Sérgio Bernardes's Brazilian Archipelago; Iñaki Echeverría Guitiérrez's recreational and ecological plan, Parque Ecológico Lago de Texcoco; System of Integrated Patches by Francisco Walker Martínez in Santiago, Chile; and Common Places, Plan Común's set of public space strategies.

Assembled Natures foregrounds projects and strategies that work against typical understandings of nature and aim to produce breakthroughs in urban transformation. It includes the Orquideorama by Plan:B Arquitectos and JPRCR Arquitectos; Guillermo Hevia García and Nicolás Urzúa's Your Reflection, a continuous mirrored pavilion; Jardín Botánico Medellín, Perímetro y Café del Bosque by Lorenzo Castro Jaramillo and Ana Elvira Vélez Villa; Gaeta Springall Arquitectos' Memorial a las Víctimas de la Violencia en México; and a visual essay on Teresa Moller Landscape Studio's Punta Pite.

The format of a monographic journal, published by Lots of Architecture and distributed globally in English, offers the opportunity to reflect on the importance of landscape as a medium for urbanism in Latin America. Featured practices and designers were invited to present their projects and to speak about their particular notions of landscape as well as their main influences, references, and the various challenges and opportunities arising in contemporary discourse.

The practices presented in this issue have pursued landscape as a representational mode that implies fiction, distance, and beauty (Fábrica de Paisaje); an opportunity for multisensorial and techno-ecological speculation (CAPA); and a space for temporary consolidation of natural, social, and urban forces that occur at various scales and with different impacts (Plan:B Arquitectos). Landscape presents an opportunity to redefine the tensions and modes of resistance between the lessons of Western models and the native environments and cultures (Francisco Walker Martínez) as well as urban expansion, land exploitation, and wildlife (Husos). It has been claimed as a medium for tackling climate change, political misinformation, social inequality, and violence (Camilo Restrepo, Enlace Arquitectura, and Iñaki Echeverría Guitiérrez) or negotiating different gradients of public space (Plan Común, Guillermo Hevia García, and Nicolás Urzúa). Landscape urbanism as a framework has also been used to spur broader inclusivity (Gaeta Springall Arquitectos).

A series of essays by Ana María Durán Calisto, Manuel Gausa, Jeannette Sordi, Ciro Najle, José Alfredo Ramírez, and Luis Callejas complement and elaborate on the issue's thematic framework. As Charles Waldheim has outlined, over the past quarter century landscape urbanism has agitated for a new vocabulary that can instrumentally advance both theory and practice. A wide-ranging discussion between Charles Waldheim, Luis Callejas, and Florencia Rodriguez reflects on the legacy of exchange between Europe and the Americas, North American disciplinary frameworks, and the influence of Latin America's design culture, both within and outside the region.

We want to express our gratitude to everyone who has contributed to the conception and realization of this project, all the authors featured in this issue, and the -NESS team. In particular, we would like to thank Charles Waldheim for his sharp-witted advice, generosity, and steady support throughout this editorial adventure.

Mercedes Peralta *is an architect and researcher currently working with Professor Charles Waldheim as a Research Associate at the Harvard Graduate School of Design's Office for Urbanization. She holds a Master of Architecture and a Certificate in Media and Modernity from Princeton University (2017), in addition to her professional diploma in architecture from University of Buenos Aires (2012). Before Harvard, Mercedes worked in New York (2017-18). She was part of the Princeton-Columbia research team for Beatriz Colomina's and Mark Wigley's Istanbul Biennial "Are We Human?" (2016) and a presenter for the 2017 ECAADE conference at Sapienza Università di Roma. Between 2010 and 2015, she worked in Buenos Aires in different design initiatives. Mercedes was a designer for Claudio Vekstein's Monumento al Grito de Alcorta, represented in the last Argentinian pavilion at the 2018 Venice Biennale. Her teaching experience includes Harvard, Princeton, and University of Buenos Aires. Her writing appears in Summa+. Her current research focuses on the intersection of architecture, landscape, and urbanism. Her latest projects include design research and editorial work on the re-use of obsolete infrastructure, mobility design, branding proposals for new cities, identity systems, and the design-curatorship of Future of the American City platform initiative*

Jeannette Sordi *is an architect and urban planner based in New York City. Until 2018 she was Associate Professor of Landscape and Urbanism at Adolfo Ibañez University in Santiago de Chile. Her PhD (UNIGE, 2013) focused on the genealogy of landscape urbanism and was published as "Beyond Urbanism" (List, 2014; Sacabana, 2017, Spanish edition). She is part of the Landscape as Urbanism in the Americas initiative since its beginnings in 2015 and co-organized conferences in Medellín, Santiago, Brasilia, Mexico, and Buenos Aires. Her main publications include the books "Andrea Branzi. From Radical Design to Post-Environmentalism" (ARQ, 2015, with Felipe Vera), "The Camp and the City. Territories of Extraction" (List, 2017, with Felipe Vera and Luis Valenzuela), and "Part-time Cities" (ARQ, 2018). She currently teaches at NYIT and is a consultant for the Inter-American Development Bank on projects in Uruguay and Argentina.*

Biological Environments

Non-human living beings are not foreign actors; rather, together with humans, they interact in a complex and constantly adapting realm. Biological Environments features diverse models of thought and practice redefining the interface between design and the environment. It embraces biologically-inspired narratives, technologies, formal and representational trends, and programs that include non-human species as co-creators. Furthermore, it highlights an assemblage of design operations linking the biosphere and the built landscape. This attention towards the biological produces thought-provoking design outcomes, reinforcing the need for both science and culture-oriented public programs.

—Mercedes Peralta

Breeding Urban Ecologies

An Ethos of Life Among Latin American Designers

ANA MARÍA DURÁN CALISTO

In his posthumous book "Brief Answers to the Big Questions" (2018), the physicist Stephen Hawking reflects on what he considers the seven most pressing issues for our time. One of them particularly resonates with Greta Thunberg's generation: "Will we Survive on Earth?" Hawking's response is crushingly pessimistic in its sci-fi optimism. He counters his belief in humanity's ability to off-set the outcomes of climate change through technological innovation with an utter disbelief in our political capacity to do so, at least in a timely fashion. In an era of denialism and alternative facts, his skepticism is justified. Could Hawking foresee the fires that would ravage Amazonia under the Bolsonaro regime—a government subservient to the *bancada ruralista* interests in dismantling forest conservation regimes, and expanding ranching and agri-business frontiers deep into the heart of Amazonia? Would Hawking be surprised to learn that there is a correlation between Trump's trade war with China and an increase in soy-bean demand from South America, more than half of which is consumed as fodder? (1)

The economic incentives of right-wing Bolsonaro are the same that led left-wing Morales, before his resignation, to promote the interests of agribusiness (biofuels/coca plantations) and ranching in the now extensively charred Chiquitanía. Bolivia's beef exports to China have been steadily growing, as have Brazil's. How many tons of carbon dioxide have been released into the atmosphere from deforestation alone in 2019?

In the face of political economy's failure to thwart the climate crisis, what does Hawking propose? A solution chillingly analogous to the one advanced by Noah in Genesis. This time around, though, the vessel is interstellar—at least, interplanetary—and meant to save a privileged few who would survive "the sixth extinction" (2) in a spatial colony. Since American scientist Gerard K. O'Neill first developed ideas for colonizing space early in the 1970s, techno-utopianism has delivered a diverse array of imaginaries. Sir Norman Foster has engaged some of the latest designs for Martian settlements, Elon Musk is leading the development of the spatial tourism industry, and China has already completed the first biological experiment on the Moon in an attempt to breed a pioneering satellite ecology. The developmental frontier advances into outer space... Yet, what happens on Earth? Are there signs of Earth-based hope? There are, plenty, and growing.

The case studies collected in this publication, for example, illustrate how design teams, governments, communities, foundations, businesses, and other forms of social organization are breeding ecologies in cities throughout Latin America. All constituencies involved in the realization of these projects are advocating for grounded and economically-sound solutions to our imminent socio-environmental problems. Each proposal understands urban nature as inextricable to the web of life: an ancient awareness of the interdependency and interconnectedness of all beings that has been recast by ecology, biology, environmental planning, landscape architecture, and other fields as a systemic understanding of the interrelations and processes that compound an ecology.

This includes an urban ecology, one that is bred, fed, or remediated within a city. Within design, this logic defies dualisms such as city-nature and expands the notion of "function" to mean, rather than segregated activity, complex systems performance of interrelated functions: environmental, social, and cultural. The optimism of professionals who work with biological

Ana María Durán Calisto *is an architect (UPenn) and urban planner (UCLA) with a background in the Liberal Arts (USFQ). In 2002, she established the design firm Estudio A0 with Jaskran (Jazz) Kalirai. Its work has been exhibited nationally and internationally in venues such as the XX Chilean Architecture and Urbanism Biennial. In 2008, Durán Calisto organized an expedition down the Napo and Amazon rivers, concerned with the environmental impact of IIRSA/COSIPLAN bi-oceanic corridors. She received a Loeb Fellowship (Harvard 2011) to develop a continental research network in collaboration with Felipe Correa. Durán Calisto has co-edited the books "Beyond Petropolis" (2015) and "Ecological Urbanisms in Latin America" (2019). Her articles and essays have been extensively published in the Americas, Europe, and Asia. Durán Calisto has been a professor at FADA-PUCE since 2002 and a visiting scholar at Yale (2020), the University of Michigan (2015), Harvard (2008), and Columbia (2007).*

paradigms of spatial design and construction is based on the conviction that human beings have had, and can renew, symbiotic—not destructive—relations with other organisms and their environment. In Latin America, this view acquires particular relevance given that more than half (seven) of twelve megadiverse nations are located in the region and that most of their economies are primarily dependent on the exploitation/export of natural resources.

Latin America is experiencing eco, geno, and epistemicide in its hinterlands, while it constructs landscape urbanisms in a plight to vindicate within urban centers the necessity to restore and care for the ecologies that enlightened Wallace, Darwin, Humboldt, and other scientists; ecologies that pulse within and beyond the city and that are being suffocated by extraction and one of its many negative externalities: massive displacement of people and the explosion of informal mantels. The case studies presented here are statements on alternative pathways towards well-being, with humans not as centerpieces but as partners in a web of life.

(1) Oliveira, Gustavo and Hecht, Susanna. Sacred groves, sacrifice zones and soy production: globalization, intensification and neo-nature in South America, in "The Journal of Peasant Studies," 43:2, 2016, pp. 251-285.

(2) For a review of past mass extinction events, and its sixth iteration in the Anthropocene, refer to Kolbert, Elizabeth. "The Sixth Extinction: An Unnatural History." A&C Black, 2014.

New public programmatic needs for the preexisting garden are organized by a spatial scheme, which was inspired by the pattern of an emblematic tree. The project mediates between landscape, art, and society.

Jardín Botánico

MEXICO

Tatiana Bilbao Estudio

Culiacán, a city in northwestern Mexico eighty kilometers from the Pacific coast, has a population of more than one million inhabitants. For more than thirty years its botanical garden has been known for its collection of over 750 species of tropical flora. Ernesto Coppel, the president of the board of trustees, began this garden with the intention of improving the city's quality of life and offering the people of Culiacán new ways of learning through experience: touching, seeing, smelling.

Besides its plant variety, this garden is unique in that it functions as a park. Visitors can enjoy various activities such as sports, picnics, or promenades through the landscape.

To develop this unique space, Coppel decided to commission a curator and thirty-five renowned artists to make site-specific art that would invite visitors to contemplate the mediation between art and society. Taller de Operaciones Ambientales (TOA) was commissioned to strengthen the botanical collection and make it one of the preeminent collections in Mexico.

Tatiana Bilbao's office was brought onto the project to develop a masterplan that would mediate between the landscape and art and also situate the service buildings needed to organize the program. The office developed a pattern by tracing the branches of one of the park's most emblematic trees onto the existing plan and mapping it into a diagram of programmatic needs. A set of buildings, including cultural areas, educational facilities, laboratories, green houses, and storage and administrative offices with public services, were distributed throughout the garden.

LOCATION: Culiacán, Sinaloa, Mexico / DATE: 2011 - 2019 (project) / SITE AREA: 10,000 sqm, 107,639.10 sf / STATUS: Built, Continued Work / MAIN ARCHITECT: Tatiana Bilbao, architect / PARTNERS: David Vaner, Catia Bilbao, architects / DESIGN TEAM: Paola Toriz, Roberto Rosales Salazar, Israel Álvarez, Mariana Tello, Lina Ruelas, Sebastián Córdova, Carlos Leguizamo, Julieta Sobral, Ana María Yumbe, Diana Figueroa, architects / CONSULTANTS: TOA, Emiliano García, Lara Becerra, Juan Rovalo, Tania Rodríguez, Claudia Rodríguez, landscape CURATOR: Patrick Charpenel / ARTISTIC COORDINATION: Cynthia Gutiérrez, Emiliano García with Tania Rodríguez and Fernando Jiménez / CONTRACTOR: Paralelo, Estandares Globales en Arquitectura, Arturo Barbosa / CLIENT: Sociedad Botánica y Zoológica A.C TEXT: Tatiana Bilbao Estudio / PHOTOS: Iwan Baan

A/B. North Access
C/D/E. Educational Services
F. Open Auditorium
G/H. Laboratories

MASTER PLAN

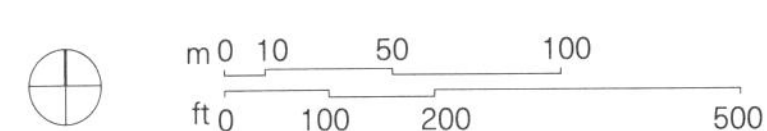

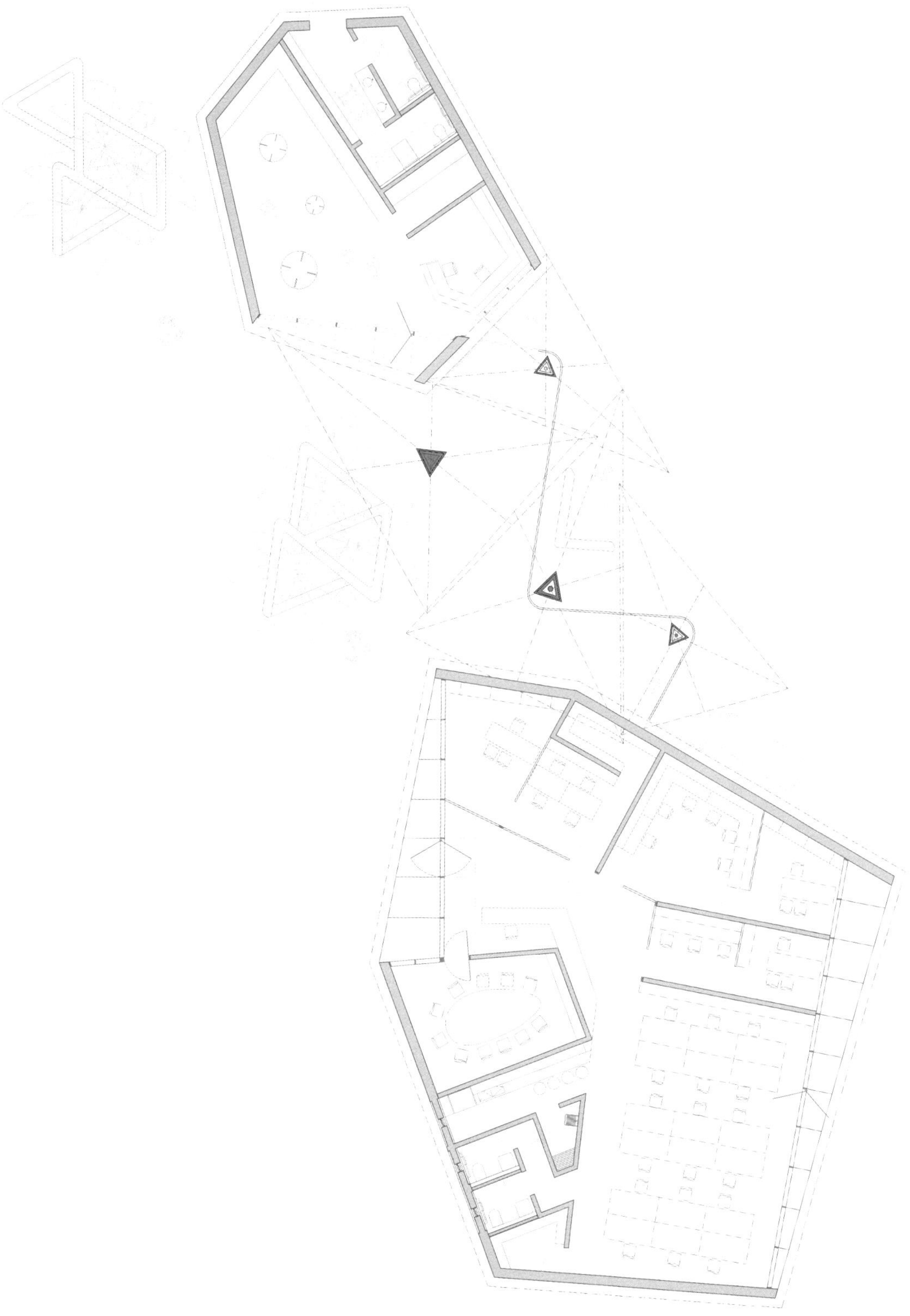

NORTH ACCESS

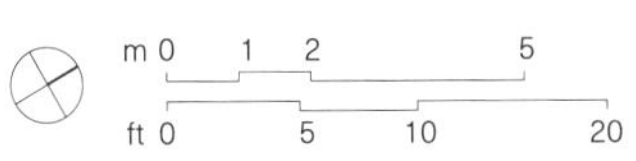

Fábrica de Paisaje dives into a fictional world where the dialectics between humans and nature pose new tools and outcomes by critically re-thinking tourism.

Supertourism

MEXICO

Fábrica de Paisaje

In our Uruguayan practice, Fábrica de Paisaje, we explore the territory as a complex field that can be transformed. We prefer to refer to the landscape rather than to other less-ambiguous constructions. The landscape is, for us, the connective tissue of the territory, neither object nor field. We conceive of our practice as a machine to produce landscapes, that is, connections—formal, cultural, aesthetic, productive, social, ethical, economic—as well as processes. To think about changes in time and adaptive systems is to think in evolutionary terms; here lies the connection between man and nature.

We try to replace an aesthetic of confrontation, based on a profoundly dialectic models (architecture and landscape, natural and artificial, man and nature), with a machinery of thought and action structured on a basis of coexistence and multiplicity that activates latent potentials and induces fictitious constructions. In this way, the name of the office, which translates to landscape factory, constitutes a real work agenda, beyond the obvious provocation that it represented when it was founded twelve years ago (and that the disciplinary evolution has clearly defined). The aim of Supertourism was to explore the fact that tourist areas are progressively found outside central regions of global economic development. The most recent updated list of the Seven Wonders of the World includes only three sites in Europe; the others are in more distant locales. This displacement is not mere coincidence. The research is based on a sequence of questions illustrated through a series of drawings and maps.

The agenda of Fábrica de Paisaje is based on three action codes: fiction, distance, and beauty. All three are firmly anchored in the specificity of landscape as an emerging and integrating discipline while, at the same time, they reclaim the great descriptors of historical landscape visions. Fiction is a trigger, generator, and sustainer of new realities and, in particular, it functions as an unfinished and personal narrative. A new landscape only exists when a story brings it to life. Distance is the capacity for alternation and superimposition of close and distant gazes, in the aesthetic and creative sense as well as in the social, economic, and political sense. Beauty is the ultimate goal of our work, recovered without prejudice while, at the same time, transformed into an active beauty.

The challenges of Latin American cities come from their territories, and these, in turn, become those of their societies. This includes, among others, building the capacity for home-grown development beyond simple productive growth without mortgaging the continent's unique environmental assets. This issue must be resolved through a redistribution of wealth, the strengthening of democracies, and the provision of opportunities for the lesser-off.

The main challenge of the discipline is surely, in this context, to articulate a practice that succeeds in addressing the banality of models that are uncritically transposed from other realities as well as from the representatives and disseminators of these models, especially the stars and the global gurus of the discipline.

The aim is also to resist local cultural operators who, with the garb of austerity as an alibi, have implanted the idea of a reborn America, full of ingenious and mechanical low-tech solutions that simplify the complex regional reality in a desperate attempt to be in the spotlight.

LOCATION: Riviera Maya, State of Quintana Roo, Yucatán Peninsula, Mexico / DATE: 2008 / AWARD: First Prize in the International Competition SUDAPAN 2008. Morphing Territorial Infra-Landscapes Tools of Production of the Landscape / STATUS: Research ORGANIZERS: Supersudaca with the support of the Instituto de Arquitectura Avanzada de Catalunya and the sponsorship of Prins Claus Fonds / JURY: Vicente Guallart, Winy Maas, Carel Weeber, José Castillo, architects / AUTHORS: Fabio Ayerra, Marcos Castaings, Martín Cobas, Federico Gastambide, Javier Lanza, Diego Pérez, architects / COLLABORATORS: Sergio Aldama, Diego Bado, Álvaro Moreno, Horacio Pérez, Adriana Puyol / TEXT: Fábrica de Paisaje

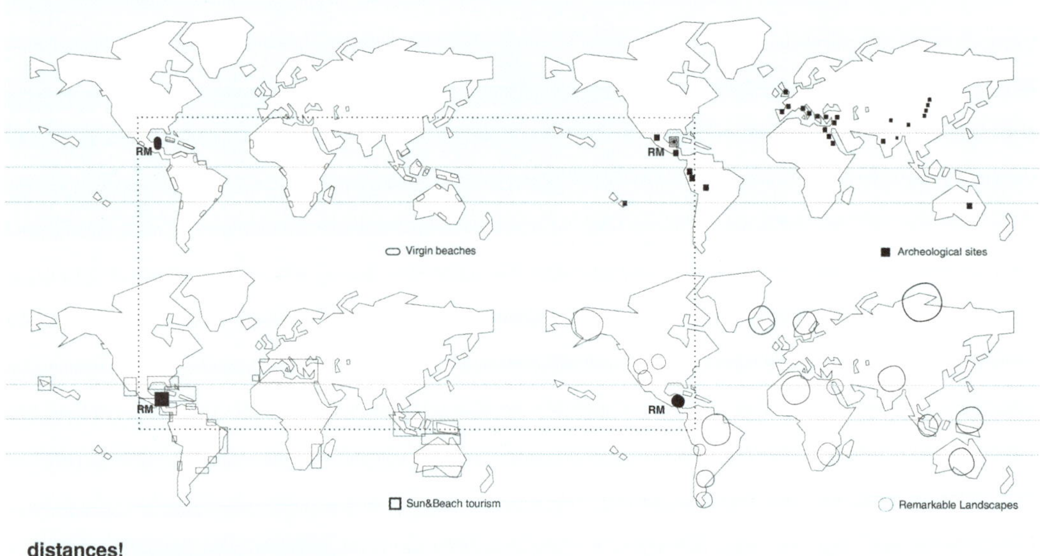

distances!

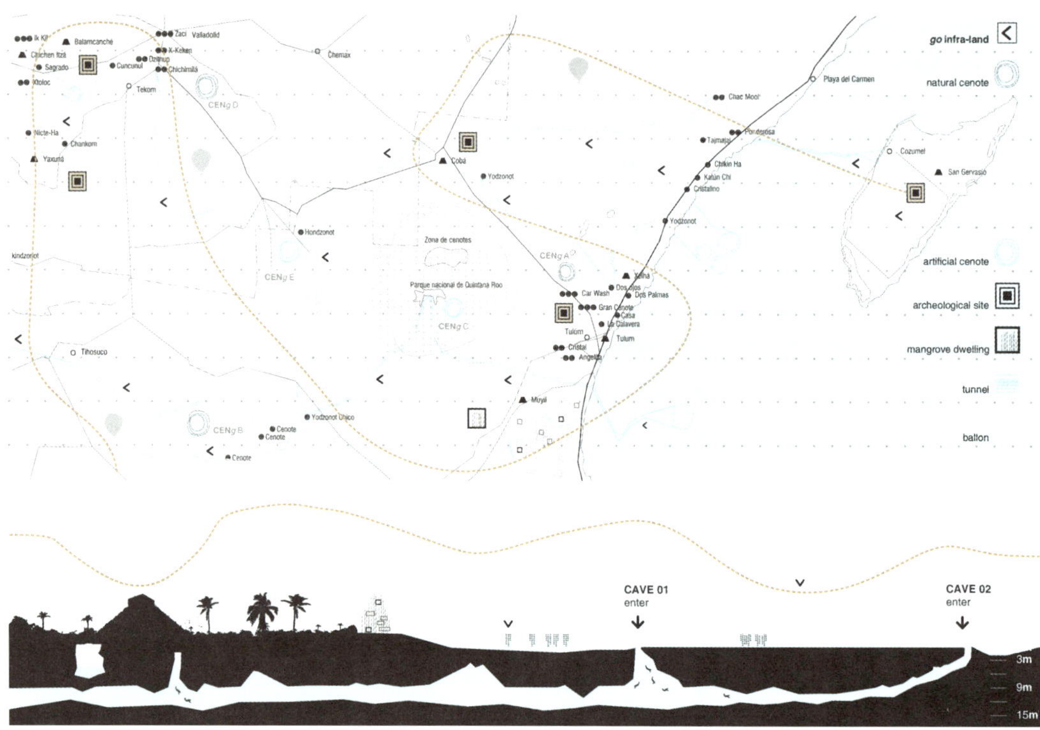

These maps introduce the notion of distances as a conceptual instrument. They render the territorial analysis and depict the specificities of each distance as well as the instruments that are developed to articulate them. Distance does not imply a lack of involvement but rather a special form of it. The maps show that micro and macroscopic oscillations involve a form of reconciliation with previously unmanageable structures as well as sophisticated and complex spatial organizations. These increasingly complex liaisons are better addressed if considered in their full dynamic scalar condition. Therefore, the landscape for Supertourism should be the result of this multi-layered vertical axis in connection with the horizontal constrictions and potentialities of the 1:1 scale, the real thing that exists beyond its representation, mapping, or cartography. The images explore operational tools or specific projects that are intended as examples of a broader field of possible actions. However, these tools are indicative rather than totalizing as it is the nature of land-factory instruments to be open, expansive, and embracing.

Artificial Islands

The Artificial Islands capture the intensity of the underwater cenotes that occasionally emerge in the Caribbean Sea, creating an underwater dwelling. This widening land-morphing strategy allows us to open the landscape not only in-land but also in-water. Supertourism* is avid of a new land, even possibly a water-land.

Edificio Jardín Hospedero y Nectarífero para Mariposas performs as a fractal hybrid unit that could potentially expand as a biological model for the city.

Edificio Jardín Hospedero y Nectarífero para Mariposas

COLOMBIA

Husos

In Husos, we consider landscape practices to be fundamental for tackling many of the environmental challenges we face in Latin America today. This includes the question of how to address the coexistence of humans and other species, which is mostly asymmetrical and often extremely conflictive. This is especially important in the Tropical Andes, where we usually work. On the one hand, the Tropical Andes tops the list of worldwide hotspots for endemism and species per surface. On the other hand, large-scale urbanization greatly impacts biodiversity. Landscape practices are especially significant in this region due to the high proportion of cities located inside or around areas with a high richness of species and endemism.

It is important to note that over seventy-five percent of Latin America's human population is found in cities, the highest proportion anywhere on Earth. Like in other places, in the Andes region, human settlements are established in proximity to natural biodiversity areas because humans have historically looked for areas rich in natural resources to inhabit, just like other species do. Therefore, today's quickly-expanding urban processes put enormous pressure on areas where the social and the natural coexist next to each other. More and more urbanization and land transformation processes, including the expansion of arable land for agriculture and other current colonial forms of extractivism, not only contribute to global warming but also reduce and limit habitats for wildlife.

In fact, the Tropical Andes area is also part of a biogeographic realm on Earth's land surface called the Neotropical region, which, according to the Living Planet Index, shows a sharp decline in species population. According to these counts, South and Central America have suffered the most dramatic reduction in species with an eighty-nine percent loss since 1970. Habitat change is often considered the primary cause of biodiversity loss globally and, in the Latin American territory, the alteration and transformation of ecosystems is identified as the greatest threat to biodiversity. Currently, habitat fragmentation, its reduction and loss, is causing a great biodiversity crisis in this part of the planet.

From our point of view, architecture, urban, and landscape practices must be understood together and not separately, as part of different scales that connect the territorial, the macro and micro territorial. Through projects such as the Edificio Jardín Hospedero y Nectarífero para Mariposas, we have tested an alternative landscape urbanism on a small scale: together with a community of neighbors, we have tried to generate a multispecies urbanism, a new relationship between humans and non-domesticated animals, including insects and different species of birds. This process has involved, first, building a vegetable membrane that attracts insects and birds, and second, publicizing the botanical experiments carried out for more than a decade in the building so as to encourage the formation of a small but very important network of environmentally-responsible gardener citizens. It was very important to attract butterflies from the region by giving them lodging and food. These insects, in addition to being very important in the ecosystem of Cali and making the building a sort of bio-indicator, operated as objects of desire or, what we usually call in our projects, Trojan horses, that is, facilitators of discussions among the neighbors and visitors of the Edificio Jardín Hospedero y Nectarífero para Mariposas. The butterflies serve as an invitation to learn about caring for biodiversity, including other less culturally desired species, such as moths, beetles, and other insects.

LOCATION: Cali, Colombia / **DATE:** 2005 (first phase) – 2010 (second phase) and ongoing / **SITE AREA:** 510 sqm, 5,489.59 sf **PROJECT:** Diego Barajas, Camilo García, architects, Francisco Amaro, biologist, building inhabitants community / **SPECIAL ASSISTANCE:** Fundación Zoológico de Cali and Lorena Ramírez / **COLLABORATORS:** Aníbal Arenas, Juan Pablo Arias, Antonio Cobo, Jahir Sabogal / **STRUCTURAL CONSULTANTS:** Jorge Mejía, Diego Gómez, Ángela María Ramírez / **CLIENT:** Taller Croquis **TEXT:** Husos / **PHOTOS:** Manuel Salinas

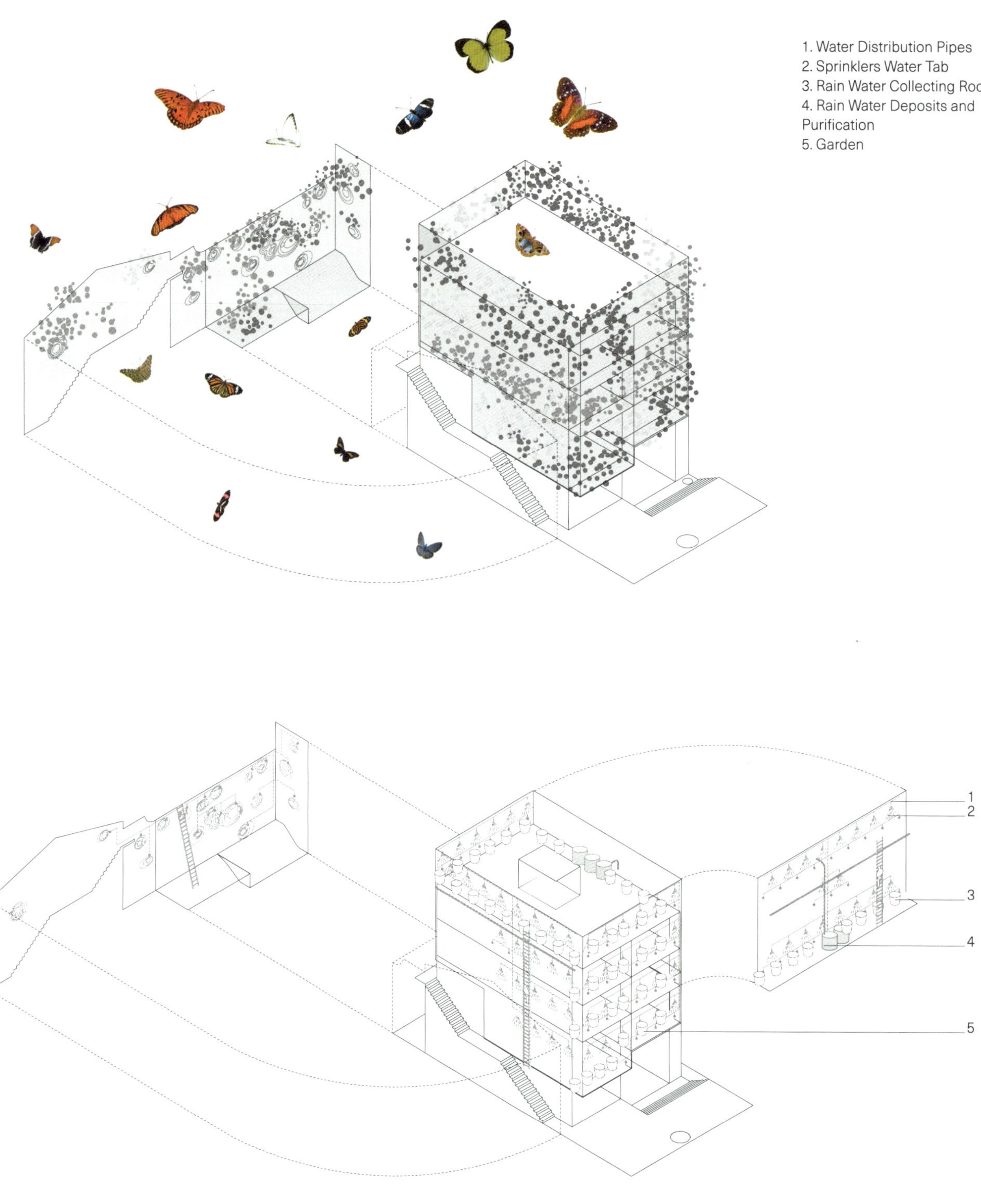

The irrigation system is composed of drip irrigation and sprinklers for the folliage. Rain water is collected on the roof and stored in water tanks located on the second floor and the terrace.

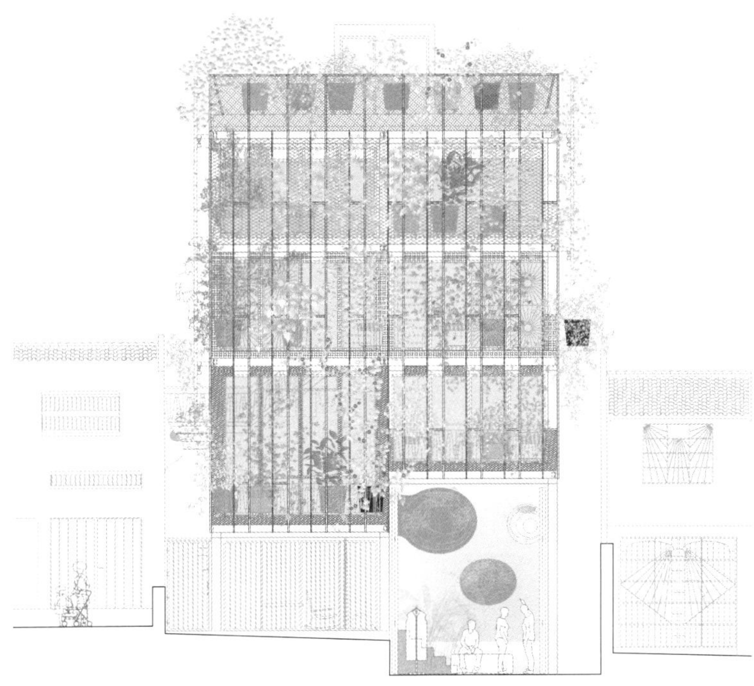

ELEVATION

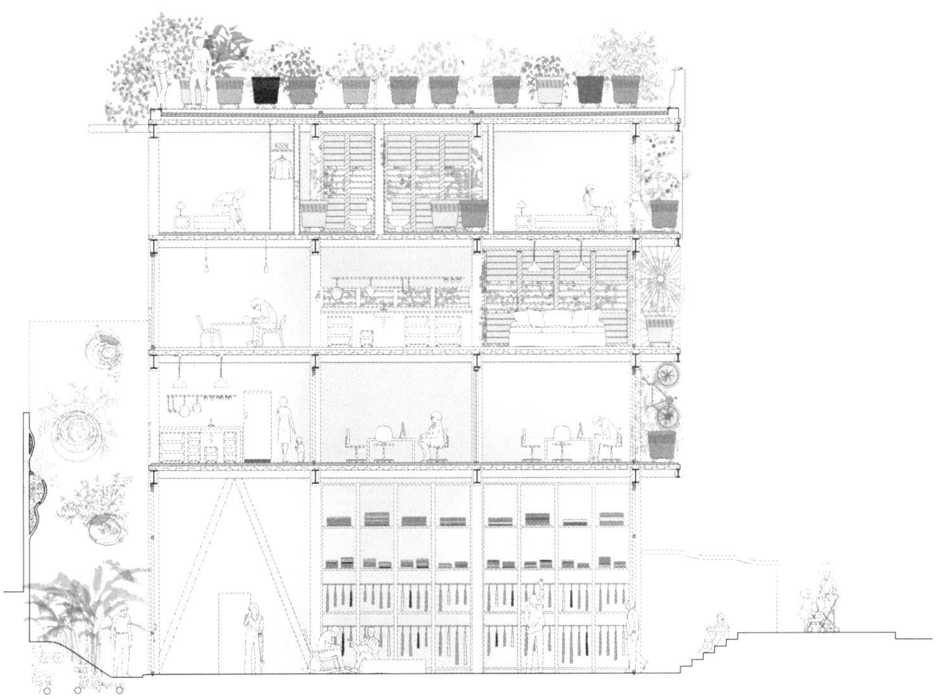

SECTION

Pharma — Park contradicts the usual narrative of black-boxed social and political policies. Instead, it uses natural resources to reimagine extraction in the Amazonian Jungle. Architecture, urbanism, and ideas of nature converge in a dynamic understanding of geography through landscape.

Pharma — Park, Landscape for Biochemical Ecology

COLOMBIA

Camilo Restrepo

The Amazon jungle and the Latin American rainforest have been presented in the public sphere as a black box; that is, it is suggested that no one outside of the forest understands its importance for human existence or its internal organization. Due to this lack of comprehension, the forest gets destroyed, invaded, and misused year after year. Also, the weak presence of government authority, development policies, and economic opportunities generates a context in which citizens see the forest as a provider of timber and a huge area apt for raising cattle, or for developing industries such as mining, oil, and infrastructure.

Due to the location of the research project and the condition of the surroundings, mainly defined by geography, we cannot escape the use or understanding of landscape. More than just a concept, landscape is the place, the site where Pharma – Park, Landscape for Biochemical Ecology takes place. Landscape is not an extra component of reality; it is its condition, where architecture, urbanism, and an idea of nature converge. In a society rich in ecosystems but poor in material (built architecture), it is hard for history to develop a narrative out of landscape. Landscape is the thread that allows us to connect the rural with urban centers, the countryside with wilderness. It is the only constant attitude for understanding our surroundings and intervening in them. It creates a certain coherence where people can meet.

The three main challenges for Latin America today are climate change, political misinformation, and social inequality. They are related and can even be understood as parts of the same problem. A lack of opportunities and social inequity lead to political manipulation and a denial or casting aside of decisions required to face the planetary reality of climate change. This leads to a high-speed exploitation of land, resources, and human groups, especially in the Global South where social consent is not part of first-priority agendas for politicians nor citizens. We lack social agreements. Under this context, the practices of architecture, urban design, and landscape appear as great opportunities, as tools or places for convergence in which social, political, economic, and environmental policies can meet in a very objective and precise way;

they can become specific and necessary projects. At the same time, from a disciplinary point of view, the question is how to make ourselves needed given the circumstances mentioned above. How much might we open the borders of the discipline so as to jump into real action, making built projects, without losing the disciplinary values of understanding networks and its effects as built environment? How can we do this while at the same time keeping our historical ethos and multiple aesthetics and maintaining our sense of belonging within a discipline that creates culture and reflects constantly on a dynamic understanding of geography?

LOCATION: Region of Antioquia, Colombia / DATE: 2011 / STATUS: Project Research / DIRECTOR: Camilo Restrepo Ochoa, architect / PARTNER: Carlos Fernando Cadavid, architect / TEAM: Mariana Mejía, Santiago Cadavid, Felipe Walter, Paulina Vargas, Paula Mesa, Julián Salazár, Manuela Castillo

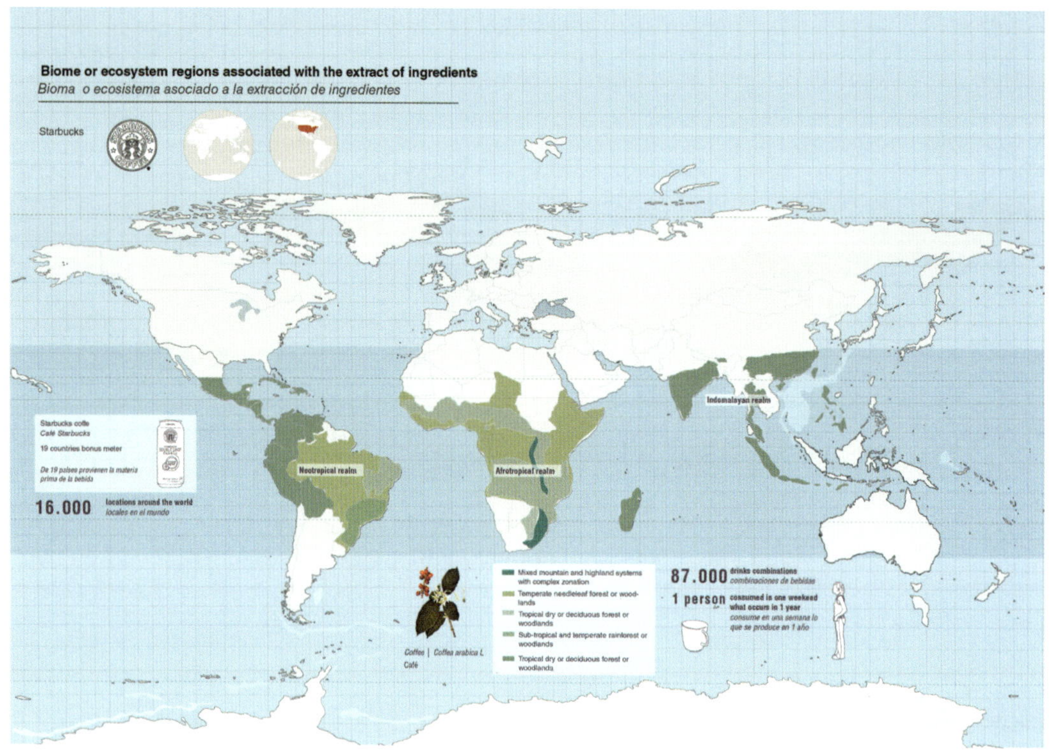

Mint, *Mentha Piperita*. Extracted for the food, cosmetics, and pharmaceutical industries.

Lemongrass, *Cymbopogon*. Extracted for the food industry.

Rose Hip, *Rosa Eglanteria*. Extracted for the food, cosmetics, and pharmaceutical industries.

Experts estimate that we are losing 137 plant, animal, and insect species every single day due to rainforest deforestation. That equates to 50,000 species a year. As the rainforest species disappear, so do many possible cures for life-threatening diseases. Currently, 121 prescription drugs sold worldwide come from plant-derived sources and twenty-five percent of Western pharmaceuticals are derived from rainforest ingredients. Less than one percent of these tropical trees and plants have been tested by scientists. By using an ethnobotanic and pharmaceutical approach to resources and a hydric system of hundreds of rivers in the Amazon as a natural highway for extraction urbanism, the project encourages the Amazonian countries (Brazil, Bolivia, Colombia, Ecuador, Peru, and Bolivia) to constitute a legal and geographical frame to establish strong and accurate policies for sustainable development and the protection of the forest and its living resources.

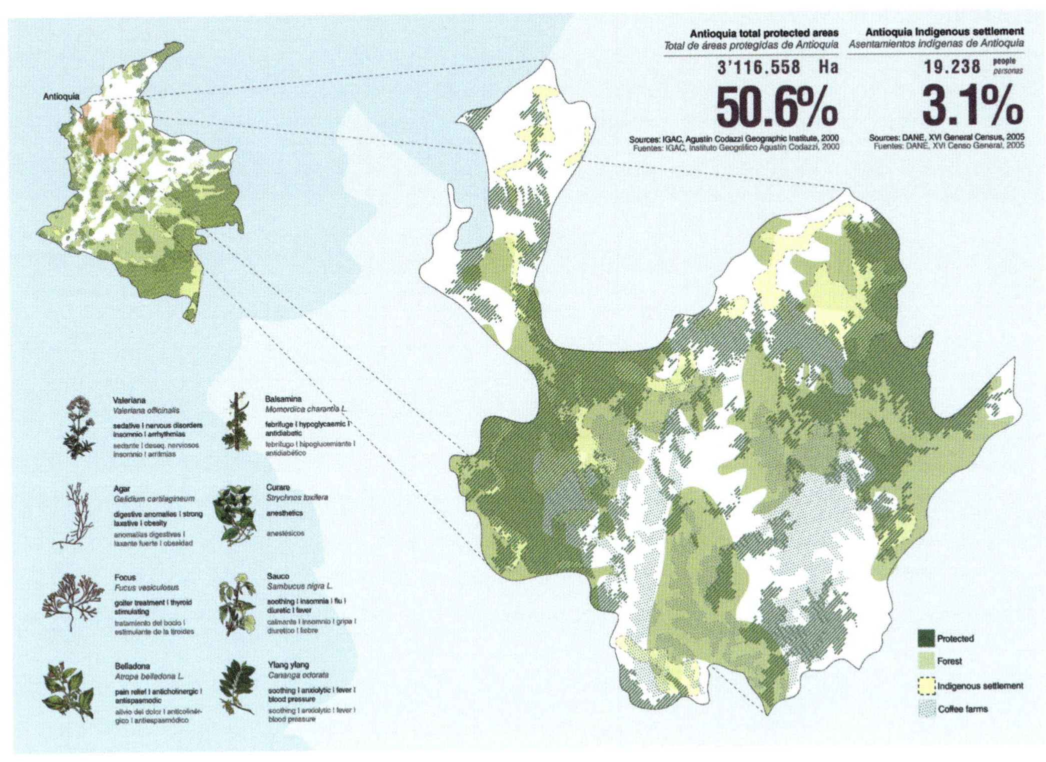

ANTIOQUIA TOTAL PROTECTED AREAS

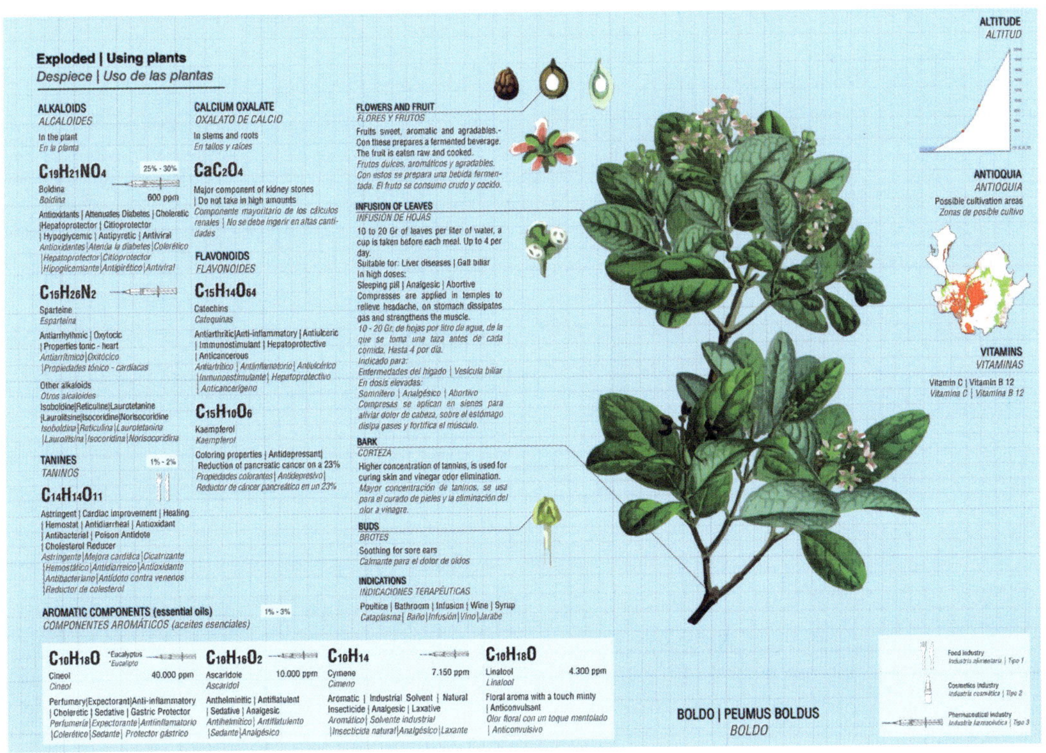

PHARMACEUTICAL APPROACH TO THE BOLDO PLANT

CAPA questions concepts of sustainability and functionality, designing forms of reciprocity between technology, landscape, and the public. The proposed garden explores the dynamic input and outcomes of variables such us soil, fertility, humidity, pollution, or even noise levels.

Multisensory Carpet

COLOMBIA

CAPA

For this sustainable gardening project, Multisensory Carpet, our working team understands the idea of landscape as the organization of the natural surroundings and the use of technological devices as well as the cooperation of citizens to ensure its functionality and sustainability. The notion of a natural environment means contemplating living beings as well as environmental and technological agents.

The project envisions landscape urbanism as a collection of small actions or projects that involve different disciplines and knowledges in order to solve a specific problem. It is the tracing of the layout and the planting of endemic species to reveal the classical beauty of the composition and the geometrical organization of the garden. The resulting forms utilize networks of both hydraulic and energy conduction. From this geometric development emerges the carpet or the platform for assembling the prototype garden that is made up of different devices to measure varying agents: soil constitution, fertility, humidity, and the amount of oxygen and contamination in the air as well as noise pollution. The gardeners that adopt this space will witness how the contemplation garden turns into an interactive, multisensory exploration. We attempt to work within a small scale in which we can experience the results of our actions, as opposed to using big surfaces or urban development. Our practice explores these kinds of projects. Problems that we explore include local issues, such as how to create security in space, and actions that involve landscape and global actions such as how to create devices that produce energy and convert this into electricity.

Given the complexity of our cities, our practice includes dynamic structures that we believe could work simultaneously with different aspects of the project. We also think that technology can be a great democratic tool in our practice. For example, in this specific project, sustainable gardening, where the users themselves can manipulate the device, will be a main component. The aesthetics of the landscape will result from the interaction between users, technology, vegetation, structures as well as intangible considerations, like economic or political factors, among others.

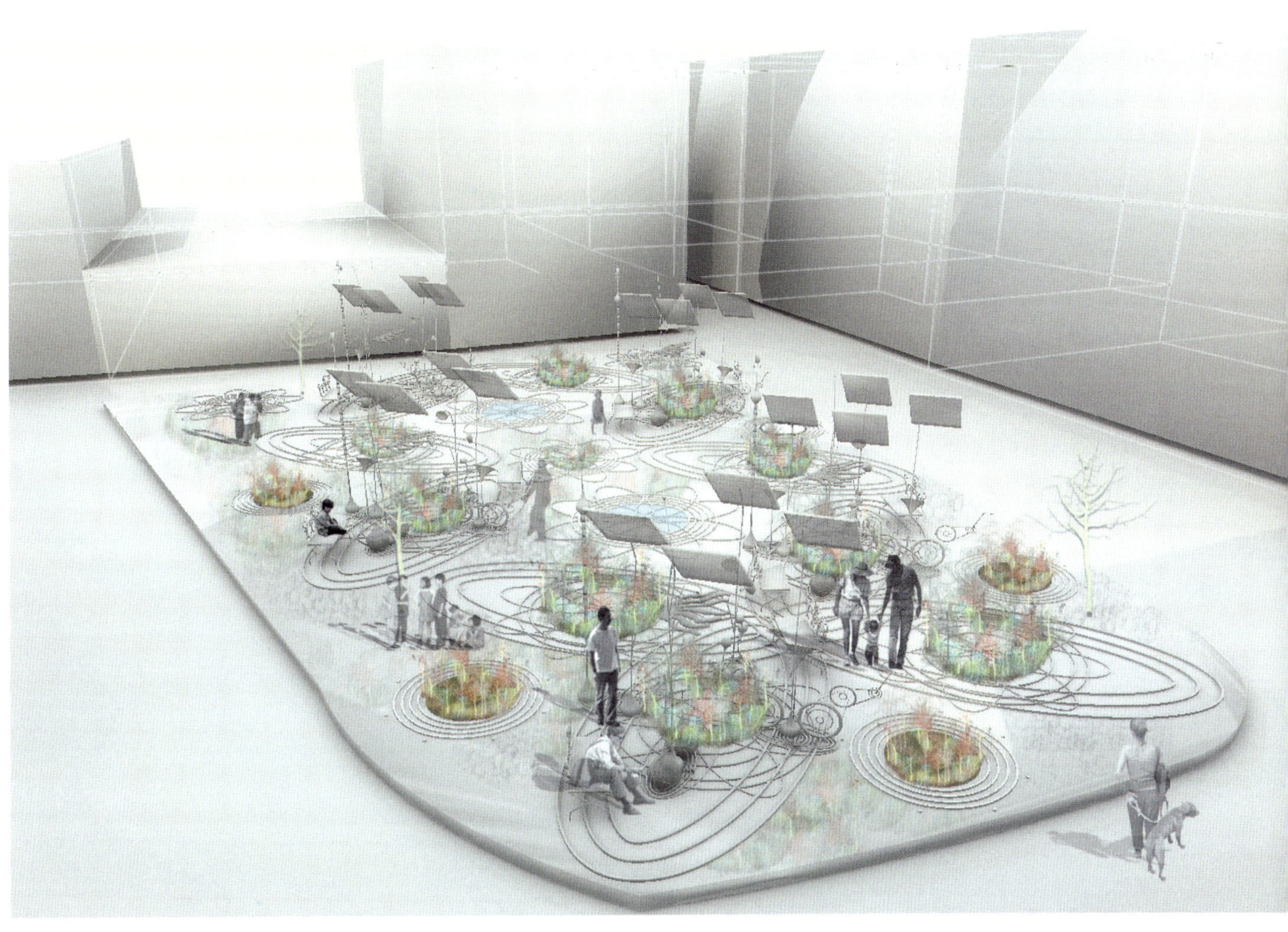

LOCATION: Santa Cruz de Tenerife and Las Palmas de Gran Canaria, Spain / DATE: 2008 / CLIENT: Art and Landscape Biennale of Canaries, Tenerife, ASA (Architecture Sustainability Association) / STATUS: Research and Representation / MAIN ARCHITECT: Catalina Patiño, Pablo Ramos, architects / PARTNER: Eliana Beltrán, architect / DESIGN TEAM: Clara Restrepo, architect, Federico López, Daniel Gómez, sound engineers, Julián Giraldo, electronic engineer, Juan Esteban Giraldo, student / TEXT: CAPA

Multisensory Carpet considers landscape urbanism as a collection of small actions or projects that involve different disciplines and knowledges in order to solve a specific problem. It is the tracing of the layout and the planting of endemic species to reveal the classical beauty of the composition and the geometrical organization of the garden. The resulting forms utilize networks of both hydraulic and energy conduction.

—CAPA

The gardens offer scientific data and inspire civil participation to optimize resources and maintain the correct bioclimatic functioning. Through swift actions, users can modify indicators to know what the right levels of each factor are for the plant's survival and preservation.

Resilient Grounds

A critical synthesis of international perspectives on landscape urbanism helps to imagine how we might more fully-realize the underutilized urban potential of territory. As our conception of the city becomes less constrained by geopolitical boundaries, new design configurations foster more radical political and social frameworks. Eschewing mimetic approaches towards nature, these projects seek to transform civic life through hybrid strategies. The demand for recreational and cultural facilities tends to catalyze the creation of public parks and multifunctional infrastructures. Such spaces allow for broader and more diverse social dynamics, enabling a more critical public awareness of ecology and inclusion, memory and place, and architecture.

—Mercedes Peralta

Landscape as Common Nexus

JEANNETTE SORDI

Over the past twenty-five years, landscape urbanism has defined a set of practices acting upon the built environment in a non-binary and dynamic way, operating beyond disciplinary divides and land mono-use. Landscape urbanism provided a framework to describe architectural and infrastructural projects that were experimenting with topography and hybrid typologies, folding surfaces, and blurring the boundaries between interior and exterior. In Europe and North America, landscape urbanism also provided a new set of practices that could help to deal with the essentially horizontal character of contemporary automobile-based urbanization and the need to reclaim vast infrastructural and industrial spaces. Large scale reclamation projects, such as Emscher Park in the Ruhr Area (1989-1999), Freshkills in Staten Island (2001-2030), the projects developed by Charles Waldheim, James Corner, or more recently, Stoss for Detroit (2001, 2012-present), suggested an approach to urban transformation based on performance, change over time, and ecological processes. An increasing awareness of the vulnerability of the planet highlights the need to adapt urban areas and shores to climate change by building spaces that absorb carbon dioxide emissions and protect and enhance biodiversity. These priorities have offered new layers and inputs to urban design and, once again, have highlighted the importance of multifaceted approaches such as those suggested by landscape urbanism projects.

Latin America presents challenges that are similar to those affecting Europe and North America, although in many cases they are exacerbated by past and present geographical and socio-political conditions. Most cities in the Americas were founded by European colonizers as outposts in the wild; centers of power and logistics backed up and sustained by a vast hinterland rich of resources to cultivate and extract. The logic of the city—organized, stable, protected from natural events—has been superimposed on that of the forest, the Pampa or the riverfront. Native populations have mostly been considered a resource themselves or, in any case, kept away from opportunities. When a large part of the population moved to metropolises like Caracas, Medellín, Bogotá, São Paulo, and Santiago during the 20th century, the contraposition between the urban and the rural, the formal and the informal, the power and the subjugated, the rich and the poor, was replicated within the space of the city. Local governments fostered a myriad of social inequalities by protecting the trade of the elite in the global market, leaving the urban realm largely unregulated and in the hands of the capitalist market. (1) Economic and social inequality translated into urban spatial segregation and unequal access to resources and public space.

The 2008 Harvard Design Magazine (HDM), "Can Designers Improve Life in Non-Formal Cities?," edited by Christian Werthmann and John Beardsley, reviewed a series of designers' attempts to upgrade informal settlements in Latin America. The projects were selected and examined through the lens of landscape: landscape can pose problems—hydrogeological risk, proximity to toxic sites, sewage canals, landfills, industrial facilities—but can also serve as an opportunity for informal settlements. (2) The journal focuses on Latin America because, in the words of the editors, the region's largest cities, including Mexico City, Buenos Aires, São Paulo, Rio de Janeiro, and Santiago have among the world's highest urban Gross Domestic Products (GDP). At the same time, in each of these sites, informal settlements were consolidating; many countries were beginning to provide residents with access to land tenure and services. These countries also had some of the world's highest levels of income and wealth disparity, making informal settlements as much an expression of inequality as of absolute poverty. (3)

In the past ten years, terms like informal architecture or tactical urbanism have become increasingly popular forms of describing interventions that offer a self-made, self-paced alternative to traditional planning and design. However, these practices often seem to ignore the fact that they are attempting to subvert neoliberal policies by deploying the same tools that they are criticizing, only on a different scale. (4) As anticipated by Christian Werthmann and John Beardsley and the work of the Latin American designers featured in the HDM issue, landscape as urbanism offers a privileged medium to soften the threshold between neighborhoods and overlap different logics in which public or private funds are invested in creating the ground for a structural change or capillary interventions. Also, throughout the continent, government policies have improved the quality of infrastructure and housing but have largely failed to modify levels of inequalities or segregation. The projects featured in this issue explore the potential of the ground as a medium to improve social and environmental resiliency; landscape as an infrastructure for civic action, exchange, and empowerment. Resilient ground suggests operations on the urban tissue that can create opportunities for civic life, connecting heterogeneous parts of the city, improving vulnerable neighborhoods, and reclaiming or protecting environmental resources.

Enlace Arquitectura, for instance, is working on creating a protocol, combining a series of strategies based on a small-scale design intervention with long-term large-scale scenarios and policies. The main question behind these projects is always the same: what if the resources that governments invest in housing were instead invested in improving and integrating public space in existing informal settlements? (5) Since 2007, Enlace Arquitectura has created over twenty punctual interventions, most of them located in the *barrios* of Caracas, Venezuela. The projects' sites include hydrogeological sensitive areas, reclaimed dump sites, or parking lots. Each design uniquely combines local materials and recycled items, such as plastic bottles and cups, and overlaps multiple activities such as a playground, movie theater, market area, or space for religious processions and community festivities. The Plaza Jorge Somaca project is one such example, designed for an informal settlement in the municipality of Libertador, in Caracas. Enlace Arquitectura worked with the community to define possible uses, removed the existing decayed pavement, leveled the ground, and created a new pavement pattern made of different concrete finishes. Steps and ramps mitigate the level changes and double as bleachers for people to sit on as they watch children play. Planters were built in the corners of the plaza to incorporate vegetation that is partly taken care of by children from a nearby school.

The projects by Metro Arquitetos Associados and Opera Publica work on the ground and topography to incorporate multiple uses and integrate different flows and meanings. Metro Arquitectos Associados' Ladeira da Barroquinha (2015), in Salvador de Bahia, Brazil, is an extension of the public space renovations for the Glauber Rocha Theater and the Gregorio de Mattos Foundation cultural area based at Barroquinha Church. The project creates a distinct topographic design that connects the two main buildings, nearby facilities, and the street market, modulating the flows of visitors and commuters. El Grito de Alcorta by Opera Publica, in Santa Fe, Argentina, celebrates the agrarian rebellion of small rural tenants known as El Grito de Alcorta (1912). The memorial actualizes this agrarian legacy by creating a daily gathering space for farmers and citizens. Interior activities that include spaces for assembly, exhibition, and an auditorium, are wrapped by a folded exterior plane and overarched by an exterior ramp and a staircase that connects the building to the pampean horizon.

In the Dom Pedro II Park, by FUPAM / LUME, H+F Arquitetos, Métropole Arquitetos, and UNA Arquitetos, landscape becomes a medium to assign multiple meanings and functions to mobility infrastructure. The masterplan is organized following three main lines of interventions: a road system, public transport, and water management. São Paulo is built on creeks and streams but these are mostly denied in the urban landscape—they are covered by roads and highways or used as open-air sewers. For decades, the municipality has invested in a private transport system, burying waterways under roads, and constructing high-rise parking lots. The region of São Paulo originally consisted of Guaraní villages of fishers and traders located at the river confluences. Today the remaining streams are used as wastewater canals and the remaining natives are living in the slums uphill. Six miles of potential shores are unreachable for the inhabitants. The Dom Pedro II Park project uses the opportunity created by the need to re-organize the road system to integrate storm-water retention and treatment pond (wetland) which, in addition to eliminating frequent flooding, organizes the redesign of public open spaces in the western strip of the park and recovers water as a hallmark of the site.

Paseo Cívico Metropolitano is the winning proposal by Groundlab, Lyonbosch+Martic, Idom, and Sergio Chiquetto for the international competition Nueva Alameda Providencia organized by the Metropolitan Region of Santiago in 2015. The project comprises the design of a twelve kilometer transport/urban corridor, from the bus station of Pajaritos, a lower-middle class area in the western part of the city centre to the more upscale areas of Providencia and Las Condes, where most commercial activities, facilities, and offices are located. Over four decades of extreme neoliberalism deeply permeated urbanization in Santiago, leading to the concentration of low-income housing at the urban fringe, fostering spatial segregation between rich and poor, and thus reinforcing unequal access to development opportunities between lower and higher income groups. On Friday, October 25, 2019, over one million people gathered along the Alameda and in Plaza Baquedano, to generate the greatest civic uprising in Chile. Although the spark that catalyzed the uprising was an increase in public transport prices, the protests were soon articulated to be against neoliberalism itself, rather than against the specific effects of it. (6) The Alameda, the site of the protest, can also be interpreted as a symbol of this rising inequality. The Alameda was designed as a green boulevard in the 19th century. In the past decades, the avenue has become the main transport axis of the city, concentrating more than one hundred public bus routes, the main metro line, and up to five lanes in each direction that are mainly occupied by private transport. Public recreational space and pedestrian paths have become extremely limited, especially in the western, poorer neighborhoods, thus reflecting the gradient of inequality that stretches west to east throughout the city.

The Paseo Cívico Metropolitano project proposes an image that could re-balance the meaning of the site for multiple groups that were left out from the decisions that created the urban space of Santiago. The project reverts the mobility hierarchy in order to privilege pedestrians and public transport, recovering the water landscapes to improve climate comfort and mitigate pollution in what is now the most trafficked avenue in the city. The Paseo Cívico crosses four different municipalities and is designed in stages, starting with the most vulnerable areas. Ironically, the project is currently under re-evaluation by the new government because of the difficulty for the existing ministries to evaluate its performance as a complex infrastructure that includes different systems of mobility, recreational spaces, and environmental benefits. (7)

These projects, like others included in this issue of –NESS.docs, suggest that landscape as urbanism can become a medium to mitigate some of the problems that emerged from the uninhibited process of exploitation that affected the continent over the centuries, addressing subjects like inequality, contamination, population displacement. Global warming, rising sea levels, storms, droughts, erosion, and the many effects of these events will only worsen in the years to come, leading to a massive loss of biodiversity, population displacement, and migration, further exacerbating inequality and access to resources. *Landscape as Urbanism in the Americas* reminds us that landscape can be a great medium to improve the environmental performance of urban design and even think of new economic scenarios based on a more efficient use of resources, but it must also be a hinge to connect the many groups inhabiting the city and transform them into a community. If we think of landscape as an entity comprising all of the genetic, dynamic, and functional relations through which the components of a territory get connected to each other, (8) we can think of landscape urbanism as a medium to orchestrate the different forces that are shaping the urban space and their evolution over time, favoring the relation and interaction among them.

(1) Castells, Manuel. La urbanización dependiente en América Latina, in "Imperialismo y Urbanización en América Latina," Barcelona: Gustavo Gilli, 1973.

(2) Werthmann, Christian and Beardsley, John. Improving Informal Settlements: Ideas from Latin America, in "Can Designers Improve Life in Non-Formal Cities? Harvard Design Magazine," No. 28, 2008.

(3) Ibid.

(4) Brenner, Neil. Is 'Tactical Urbanism' an Alternative to Neoliberal Urbanism?, quoted in Federighi, Valeria. The Informal Stance, in "Post 24, AR+D," 2018.

(5) Silva, Elisa. "Enlace Arquitectura. Pure Space," Barcelona: Actar, 2019.

(6) Vergara-Perucich, Francisco and Boano, Camillo. From Flowers to Bella Ciao, The Origins of the Chilean Revolt, in "Il Manifesto," October 30, 2019, available online at global.ilmanifesto.it

(7) Allard, Pablo. La nueva 'Nueva Alameda', in Consejo Políticas de Infraestructura, June 04, 2019, available online at infraestructurapublica.cl

(8) Farinelli, Franco. L'arguzia del paesaggio, in "Casabella," 575-76, 1991, pp. 10-12.

This project is conceived as a piece of urban landscape that deals with questions around history, inclusivity, geographical conditions, and the technical knowledge that supports a future image of the city.

Paseo Cívico Metropolitano – Alameda Providencia Corridor

CHILE

Groundlab, LyonBosch+Martic, Idom, Sergio Chiquetto

Landscape is defined by the geographer Denis Cosgrove as "a historically specific and consciously constructed way of seeing and controlling the world... developed by, and meaningful to, certain social groups.... (1)" This definition underpins our practice, our reflections, and our thinking of the world and the way we intervene in it through our projects. For instance, in the Alameda Providencia project in Santiago we considered Alameda Avenue to be a historically-constructed urban landscape developed by, and mainly benefitting, certain social groups, which, over time, helped to produce its contemporary image. Today The Alameda Providencia is the main civic and transport axis of the city, concentrating more than one hundred public bus routes and some of the most remarkable monuments, public buildings, and institutions in the country. Despite this, The Alameda Providencia's landscape has privileged private transport over public mobility and pedestrians, accentuating inequalities. During a period of modernization, the construction of the metro system uprooted many of the alamos that gave the area its symbolic name, Alameda. This exacerbated more the divisions and inequalities between public and private transport, reducing its usage as a public space, especially in the western areas of the avenue.

These factors had to be understood and rethought in order to come up with a new image that might rebalance the landscape and incorporate social groups that had been historically left out or granted little or no voice in the space's production. The questions we asked ourselves were, from a social perspective, what kind of landscape image do we want to produce? What kind of landscape techniques would be required to achieve that image? We came up with some technical solutions: inverting the pyramid of mobility to privilege pedestrians and public transport, recovering water landscapes and ensuring forestation of the avenue to allow for shade and maintenance and provide comfort to pedestrians and other users. However, what was crucial to us was to understand the historical and geographical conditions that had generated this landscape: how did this site come to be, and how could knowledge of the site, including technical knowledge, be used to evolve and project its future image? We proposed to make the landscape of

the Alameda Providencia more inclusive of a wider and collective set of social groups in Santiago through the design and production of what we call a Paseo Civico Metropolitano. (2)

Our practice and idea of landscape is based on research produced by the Landscape Urbanism Graduate Program at the Architectural Association (AALU) in London. AALU has developed its understanding of landscape as a model through the lens of territory. However, territory is a larger framework than landscape. Territory allows us to understand the relationship between places and power and the ways they shape the world and our practice. We consider Stuart Elden's definition of territory as "a bundle of political technologies," (3) and view landscape as one of these, available to shape the world. Douglas Spencer and Clara Oloriz call landscape a political aesthetic machine, (4) or a way and means through which we create designed environments that are meaningful to certain social groups (as explained above by Cosgrove's definition of landscape). In this way, territory includes not only landscapes but also all places that have not been designed but are the product or by-products of many landscapes (particularly city landscapes) such as productive lands, logistical zones, extraction areas, infrastructural works, etc. Our practice is preoccupied with finding and designing alternative forms of urbanization that are based on landscape-oriented models. However, landscape as urbanism, in our case, is seen through a power-place relation that territory brings about and that is fundamental for offering the necessary impacts and transformations that contemporary urbanization requires.

The main challenge for designers in Latin America, and other world regions, is our exclusive focus on cities.

LOCATION: Santiago, Chile / **DATE:** 2015 (competition), 2019 (project), 2019 (construction) / **SITE AREA:** 12 km length / **CLIENT:** Regional Government of Santiago, Chile / **STATUS:** First Prize / **DESIGN TEAM:** Groundlab (LyonBosch+Martic, Idom, and Sergio Chiquetto, architects) / **TEXT:** Groundlab

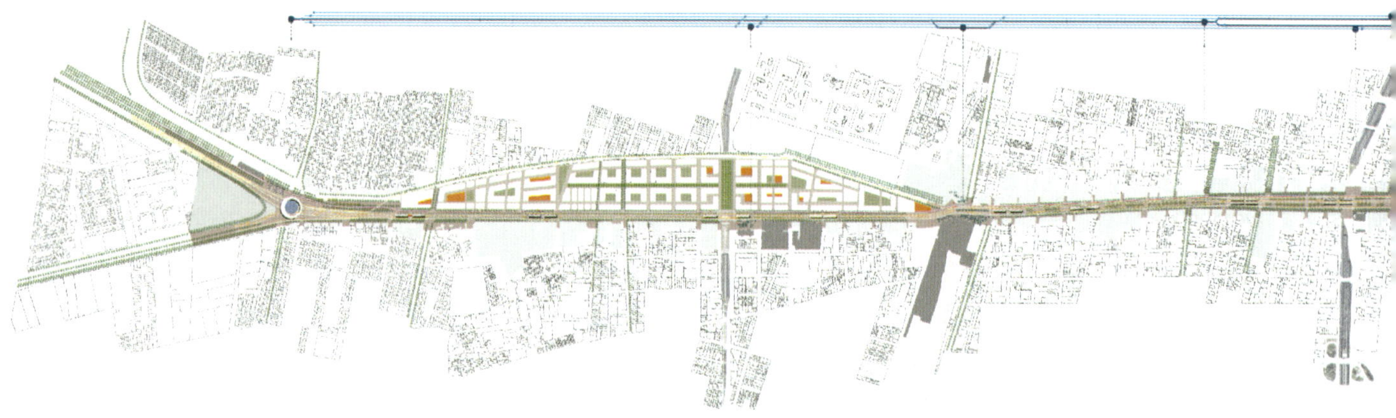

GENERAL PLAN

Looking at them as the main aim for design practices relegates the landscapes and territories from which these cities depend and directly relate to. The challenge of our practice is to unveil and reveal the way these landscapes and territories have been produced, beyond city boundaries, whether it is through extractive, productive, infrastructural, conservational, or logistic activities, and to explore the level of interdependency they have with cities. This interdependency is usually veiled behind aspirational models of cities, such as the sustainable city, the smart city, the green city, the resilient city, and so on. Understanding, thinking about, and revealing this interdependency will profoundly transform the way we design and built our urban environments. In this way, we favor Neil Brenner's Planetary Urbanization (5) over the Urban Age (6) narrative. Planetary Urbanization is seen as a process that works and redefines the urban across the entire planet, while the Urban Age looks at the city as an ideal model to be followed and revered. We understand urbanization as a series of processes, with a variety of intensities, enmeshed within the whole planet. Given the current climate crisis, it is paramount to not only understand and reflect on this thinking but also to design and visualize it. To project new and radical urban futures for Latin America and beyond, we need to reveal local, regional, and planetary interconnections and consequences that challenge the profession. These revelations will help us propose, design, visualize and, ultimately, produce new relations between nature and society.

(1) Cosgrove, Denis E. "Social Formation and Symbolic Landscape," University of Wisconsin Press, 1998.

(2) Details of the project at groundlab.org

(3) Elden, Stuart. "Land, terrain, territory," in Progress in Human Geography, 34 (6), 2010, pp. 799–817.

(4) Olóriz Sanjuán, Clara. "Landscape as Territory." Actar, 2019.

(5) Brenner, Neil. "Implosions/Explosions: Towards a Study of Planetary Urbanization", 2014th edition, 2014.

(6) Brenner, Neil and Schmid, Christian. "The 'urban age' in question', International Journal of Urban and regional research," 38(3), 2014, pp. 731–755.

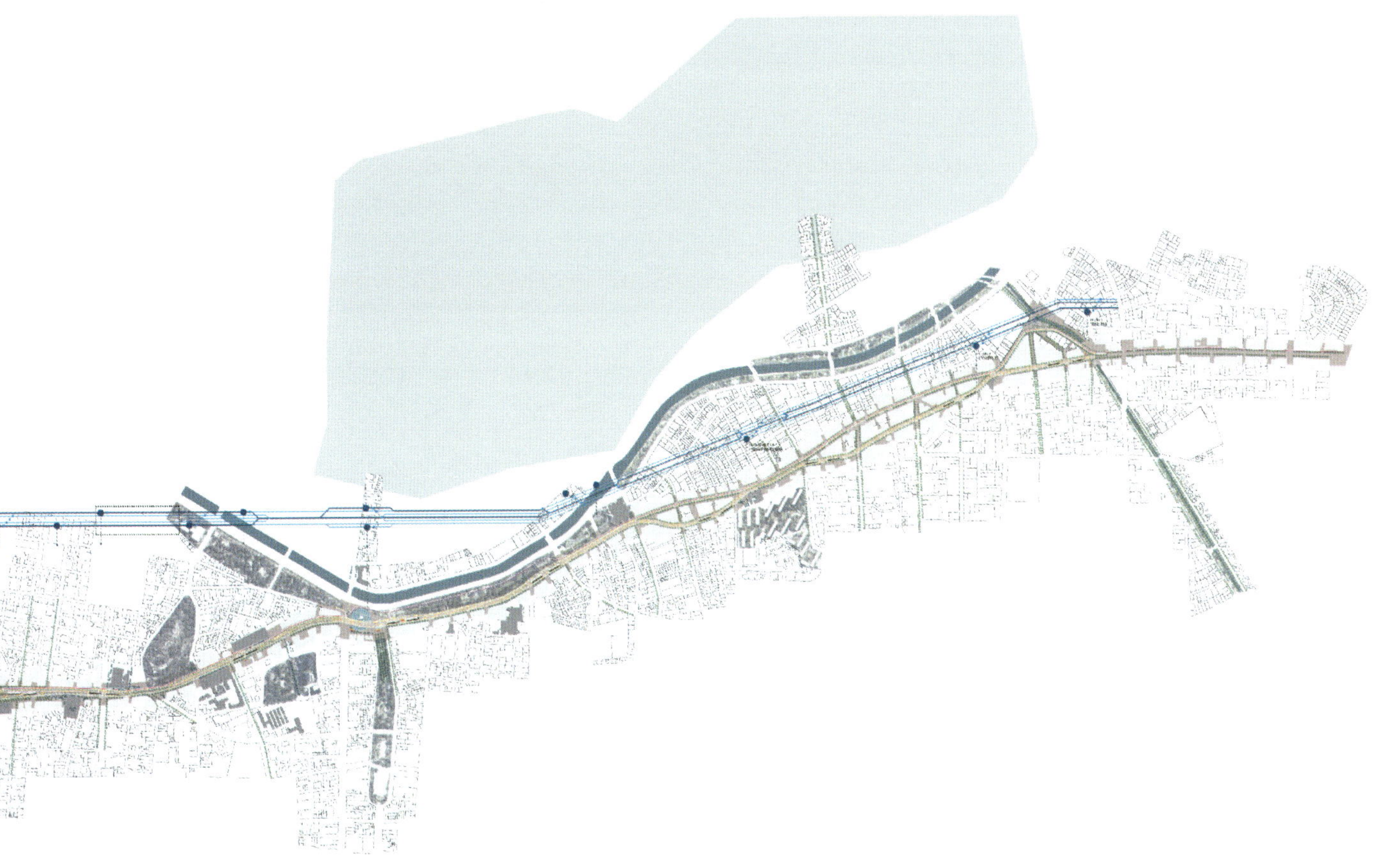

The pyramid of mobility has been inverted in order to privilege pedestrians and public transport, recovering water landscapes and ensuring forestation of the avenue to allow for shade and maintenance and provide comfort to pedestrians and other users.

—Groundlab

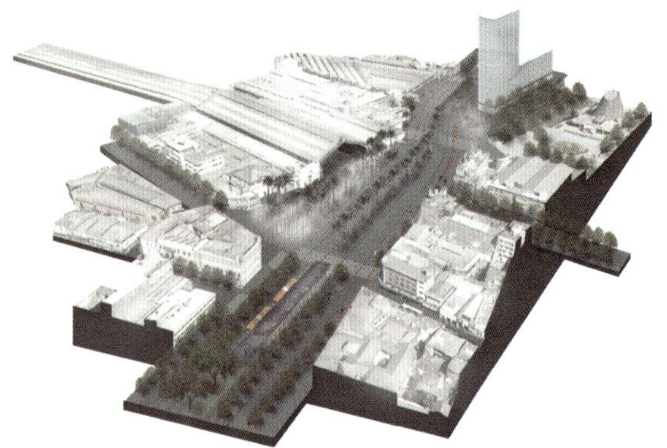

ESTACIÓN CENTRAL

ESTACIÓN TOBALABA

PLAZA BAQUEDANO

PUBLIC TRANSPORTATION STOP

ESTACIÓN CENTRAL

AVENIDA PROVIDENCIA

The design for this park engages with preexisting complex road infrastructures and traffic flows to use mobility to its advantage. In consequence, the project intends to resignify that historical landscape.

Dom Pedro II Park

BRAZIL

FUPAM / LUME, H+F Arquitetos, Metrópole Arquitetos, UNA Arquitetos

Situated on the Tamanduateí River floodplain and inaugurated in the 1920s as the main public leisure space in the historic center of São Paulo, Dom Pedro II Park succumbed, during the 1960s and 1970s, to the disastrous implementation of road infrastructures designed to accommodate the rising metropolitan traffic flows. These projects included the East-West Express diametric connection, an elevated metro station, two busway stations, and the largest urban bus terminal in the country.

Transformed into a large residual and discredited roundabout with no local life, the area now faces the challenge of acquiring new meaning, one that regains its historical importance and that dialogues with its contemporary functions.

This masterplan attempts to avoid the nostalgic approach of previous projects that sought to restore the bucolic park that was originally implemented. The project resignifies landscape through the potential of this great mobility node, integrating it with other functions and scales through the physical reconfiguration of its infrastructures and breaking the dichotomies between form and function, beautification and utilitarianism, metropolitan scale and local scale.

The masterplan is structured through three lines of intervention. First, the plan incorporates and extends an existing project that looks to lower a section of Estado Avenue to enable the replacement of four existing transverse viaducts, expanding and qualifying local permeability and accessibility. Second, all systems are reorganized and integrated through a new intermodal station located next to the existing metro station, improving its articulation as well as its accessibility to the historical city center. The new station organizes a large courtyard providing greater comfort for users and a more urban relationship with its immediate surroundings. And third, relating more precisely to water management, a storm water retention and treatment pond (wetland) is proposed that, in addition to eliminating frequent flooding, organizes the redesign of public open spaces in the western strip of the park and rethinks water as a hallmark of the site.

In addition to the proposals for the park itself, studies were made for the transformation of two strategic sectors located in its surroundings and from which the renewal process would begin. The proposed interventions were organized in a sequence of implementation phases in order to achieve impacting results in the short, medium, and long terms and thus inducing their continuity in the future with political and administrative transitions.

LOCATION: São Paulo, Brazil / DATE: 2009 (competition), 2011 (project) / SITE AREA: 1,000,000 sqm, 10,763,910.41 sf / CLIENT: City of São Paulo – Department of Urban Development / STATUS: Project / DESIGN TEAM: FUPAM (José Borelli), LUME (Regina María Prosperi Meyer, Marta Dora Grostein, Laboratório de Urbanismo da Metrópole, University of São Paulo), H+F Arquitetos, Metrópole Arquitetos (Anna Helena Villela, Eduardo Ferroni, Pablo Hereñú), UNA Arquitetos (Cristiane Muniz, Fábio Valentim, Fernanda Barbara, Fernando Viégas) COLLABORATORS: Bruno Nicoliello, Cecília Torres, Liz Arakaki, Renan Kadomoto, Thiago Moretti, Tammy Almeida, Carolina Yamate, Carolina Domshcke, Felipe Chodin, Karina Kohutek, Luisa Fecchio, Natália Tanaka, Nike Grotearchs, Ana Paula de Castro, Carolina Klocker, Eduardo Martorelli, Fabiana W. Cyon, Filipe dos Santos Barrocas, Igor Cortinove, Miguel Muralha, Roberto Galvão Júnior, Bruno Gondo, Henrique te Winkel, Luccas Matos Ramos, architects / CONSULTANTS: Hidrostudio, Water Management, VETEC, Traffic Engineering TEXT: Design team

The study developed for the park's west sector includes a set of nine blocks along the street 25 de Março, between Ladeira General Carneiro street and Avenue Rangel Pestana. Considering the underutilization of an extremely important area of the city and the impact of the plan's actions, an urban transformation strategy is developed based on immediate application, public actions, and short- and medium-term complementary initiatives associated with the private initiative.

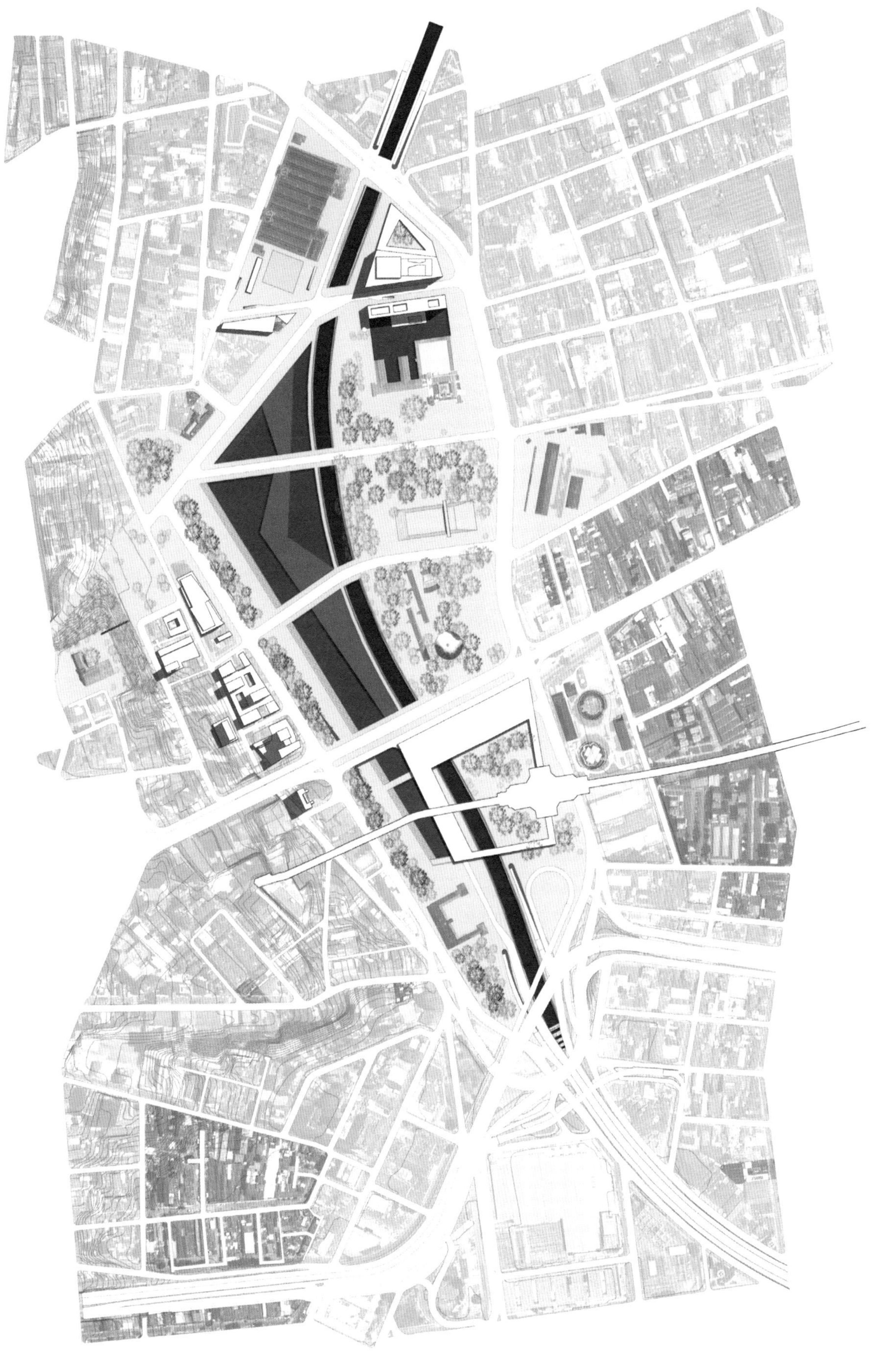

SITE PLAN

Ladeira da Barroquinha manages to define borders by being fixed to the ground without occupying space. Its territory is left open to be filled with its neighborhood uses, creating a small-scale intervention with urban qualities.

Ladeira da Barroquinha

BRAZIL

Metro Arquitetos Associados

The urbanization project of the Praça do Cinema Glauber Rocha square and the Ladeira da Barroquinha takes into consideration the importance of built heritage; it looks to reconcile the diverse present and desired uses for this important axis in the Historic Center of Salvador de Bahia. The city's context—it is the oldest city in Brazil with a strong history due to its colonization by the Portuguese—inspired the use of Portuguese stone. We approached the project through the city's identity, linking the landscape with the cultural context.

As architects, we are always looking beyond the site itself. We study the surroundings and consider what exists in order to make a project coherent with its environment; the landscape is present in all of our projects. Sometimes this link between what is intended to be built and what already exists is made through the consideration of analogous elements, using drawing, material, or a leading idea to build these similarities, while at other times it is explored through contrasts.

Even though we have some important large-scale urban projects in Brazil, such as Aterro do Flamengo, landscape design is often a missing component, specifically for smaller scale projects. There are only a few examples of projects that consider the neighborhood scale, which allows professionals to develop a system capable of impacting daily life.

In Latin America, most of the problematics or preoccupations related to social, economic, environmental, and political challenges are new, due to costs and public policies. However, in general, there is a specific context from which the projects emerge, and throughout their development, the experience is generally positive. In our case, the project source is inexistent, and therefore a culture around landscape is also missing. Bahia has a build-your-own-sidewalk culture, and the whole city reflects this through its fragments; it is visually and physically disconnected. Thus, the challenges are numerous and the future will require large investments, both private and public, in urban landscape design. These investments, however, should be focused on the neighborhood scale, with a masterplan that considers

the history and uses of the area—only then will the city become more pleasant for pedestrians. The design itself, the materials, and the consequent size of the investment, should be of similar quality to other private sector projects. After all, the material resistance and design of public space are decisive for the longevity and impact of the city. No matter how adept we are at alternative urbanist practices, in order for these practices to be feasible a very consistent urban foundation is necessary—something that is not usually the case in Brazilian cities.

LOCATION: Salvador de Bahia, Brazil / DATE: 2013 (competition and construction) / SITE AREA: 2,440 sqm, 26,263.94 sf / STATUS: Built / ARCHITECTURE DESIGN: Metro Arquitetos Associados / PROJECT MANAGER: Martin Corullon, Gustavo Cedroni, architects COLLABORATORS: Marcelo Macedo, Miki Itabashi, Flavio Bragaia, Isadora Marchi, Luis Tavares, Rafael de Sousa, architects / CONSULTANTS: Ricardo Heder, light design, Ricardo Vianna, landscape, P.K.M., and Usina de Projetos, infrastructure / TEXT: Metro Arquitetos Associados PHOTOS: Ilana Bessler

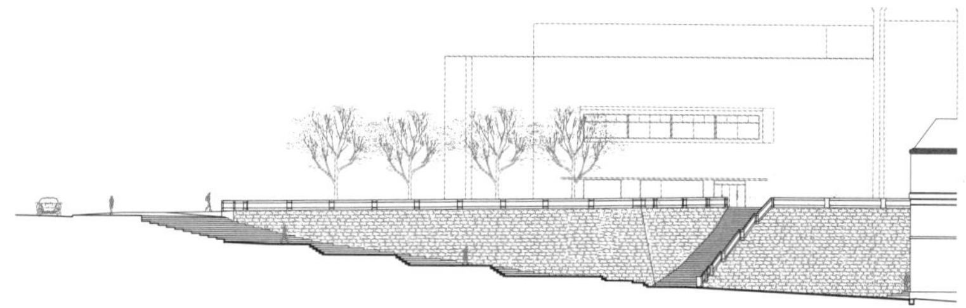

SECTION

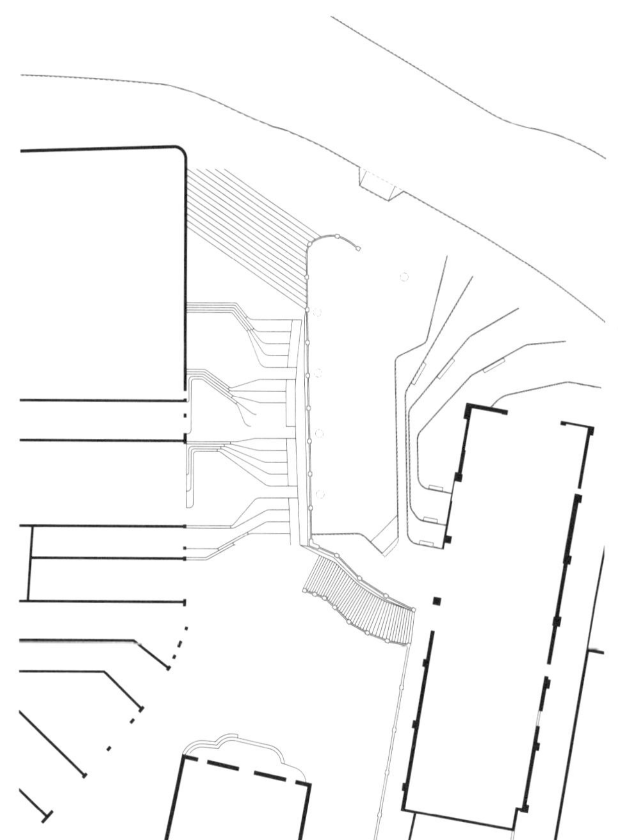

SITE PLAN

m 0 3 6 15
ft 0 10 25 50

3321 - 4779

This Memorial Space and Monument to the 100th Anniversary of the Alcorta Farmers Revolt explores relation between landscape and portrait.

El Grito de Alcorta

ARGENTINA

Opera Publica

A tension between memorial space and monument defines this work. The project explores the landscape and the portrait, or more generally, the field and the object, in pictorial terms. The task was to avoid landscape and portrait as separate entities and therefore confuse them as one. This can also be found in my research and practice platform, Opera Publica (public works), that explores the intensity of a thing, or building with the res-publica or common good in mind. By encompassing a political dimension of architecture, one that is inclusive of public interest issues such as the contemporary framework of the megapolitan city, Opera Publica uses architectural materials to activate the micro-scalar urban territories that negotiate physical, environment, and societal struggles. The works speak, from architectural locality to environmental sociology and urban ecology, fostering socially-entrenched urban infrastructure and applying disciplinarily engaged activism through architectural and social premises across multiple scales. Opera Publica seeks fine-tuned proximity to reanimate public life, building on narrative, structure, citizenship, and landscape—the character and shape of the land to which people belong, or the vital breath of the everyday, in both the singular and the ordinary of the universal scape of the city's realm.

This work celebrates the rural tenants—mostly Italian and Spanish immigrants—who engaged in an agrarian rebellion known as El Grito de Alcorta (1912); it evokes the farmers, their work and struggles, the use and possession of the land, and the cooperative nature that emerged. It also actualizes them in a daily gathering space for farmers and citizens, overwriting the passive, reverent monuments of the past. Only four large exposed concrete foundations remained in the bare terrain, monumental sculptural figures built in the Socialist Realism Soviet style on the 50th anniversary of the rebellion. In this project, the area was turned into a building program capable of hosting small cultural gatherings, functioning as a civic plaza, an auditorium, a gallery, or an historical interpretation center. The interiors' intense and intimate scales are housed by an extensive, folded exterior plane structured by large steel rhythmic porticos, inclined frames, and modular rugged panels. This screen carries

the expressive aesthetic content while articulating its monumental scale as a classic scenery to be seen along the trails that circulate nearby.

The massive relief, resembling historic stockpiles of burlap sacks, materializes through locally-crafted panels made out of resin and reinforced with fiberglass and crude burlap molded on geometrically pixelated wooden forms. The west pavilion, containing offices and public toilets, is a reinforced concrete structure with steel profiles emerging from the plowed earth. It frames the vast horizon and Pampean sunsets, with its descending terraces accessed by the exterior ramp along the main screen and a staircase along the stepping. Rough textures at different scales reveal a textile and tactile grain that resembles the labor engraved by the agrarian workers on the land, their tanned skins rugged with wrinkles and cracked by the sun, their clothing, and the rough bags piled up in the storage. A free-standing wall and horizontally extruding porticos conjoin to form continuous sections. The fluted surface unfolds beyond the building and the sectioning of the metal panels unites it with the horizon. The exterior Pampas trees are connected intimately with the interior, forming its plywood furniture and extending its exhibition surface by wrapping the auditorium in furrowed boards.

LOCATION: Route 90 Kilometer 78, Commune of Alcorta, Santa Fe Province, Argentina / DATE: 2011 (competition), 2018 (construction) SITE AREA: 7,500 sqm, 80,729.32 sf / BUILT AREA: 400 sqm, 4,305.56 sf / CLIENT: Argentine Agrarian Federation, Government of Santa Fe Province, Commune of Alcorta, Government of the Argentine Republic / STATUS: Built / ARCHITECTURE DESIGN: Estudio Claudio Vekstein, Opera Publica / PROJECT MANAGER: Carolina Telo, architect / PROJECT ASSISTANTS: Mariana Pons, Pedro Magnasco, Mercedes Peralta, Martin Flugelman, Santiago Tolosa, Stephen Wanderer, Susan Franco, Alisha Rompre, Elizabeth Menta, Dolores Cremonini, Maca Cerquera, Pamela Galán, Shaghayegh Vaseghi, architects / CONSULTANTS: Elena Rocchi, Lucia Schiappapietra and Teresa Rozados, Landscape Architecture Consultants; Tomás del Carril and Javier Fazio, Structural Consultants; Mark West and Ronnie Araya, Paneling Consultants; Giuliana Nieva, Lighting Consultant / CONSTRUCTION MANAGEMENT: Province Department of Architecture and Engineering (DIPAI), Special Projects Unit, Ministry of Public Works and Housing, Santa Fe Province / PHOTOS: Federico Cairoli (pp. 71 and 74), Sergio Gustavo Esmoris (p. 73)

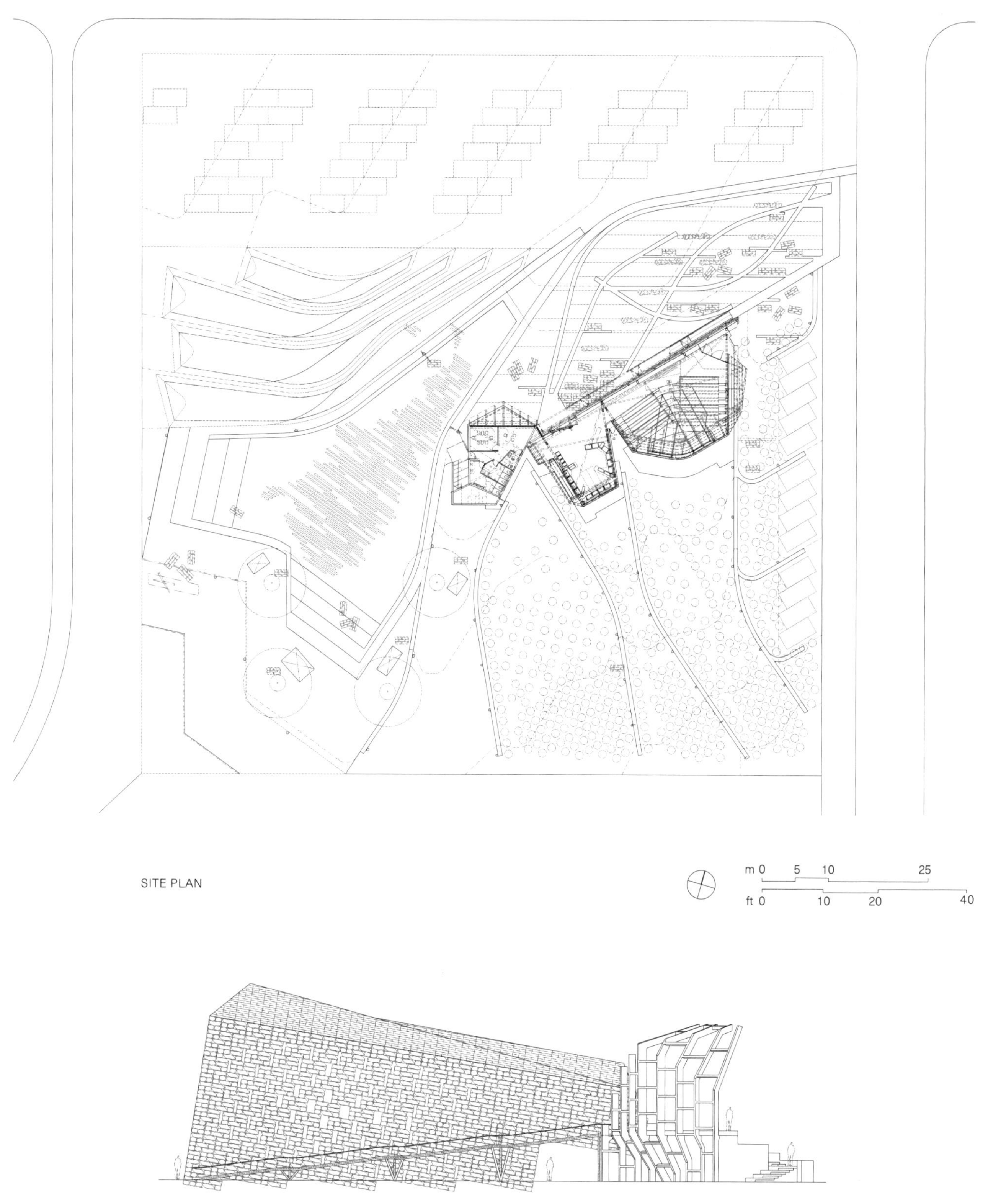

SITE PLAN

NORTHWEST ELEVATION

This intervention deals with the informal by focusing on defining the groundwork and imagining new ways to re-signify and give value to open space.

Plaza Jorge Somaca

VENEZUELA

Enlace Arquitectura

Chapellín is an informal settlement in the Libertador municipality in Caracas. It is a community that has existed for over eighty years. Nestled between the neighborhoods of La Florida and the Caracas Country Club, it developed along the Chapellín creek over the course of several years and is a dense and well-consolidated community.

The not-for-profit organization, Caracas Mi Convive, has been working with the community for several years. Enlace Arquitectura was asked to join them in the construction of a public space project funded by the Swiss Embassy in Venezuela. By working with the community through neighborhood assemblies, the team could come to understand and decide where the community would like to see their public spaces transformed and determine the types of activities that those spaces should facilitate. A focal space along the main *barrio* road was chosen. This area used to have a one-meter level change in the middle, making it unsuitable for ball games or large gatherings and processions. The pavement was in poor condition and the water was filtrated under the surface. The project removed the existing decayed pavement, leveled the ground, and created a new pavement pattern with different concrete finishes. Steps and ramps mitigate the level changes and double as bleachers for people to sit on as they watch the children play. Planters were built in the plaza's corners to incorporate vegetation into the space. The children from a nearby school planted beans and medicinal species and are responsible for watering them.

Plaza Jorge Somaca was named after a longtime Chapellín neighbor who was the coordinator of the Asociación de Jóvenes Unidos and a very important advocate and supporter of the project. Sadly, he passed away before the plaza was inaugurated; the space was named in his memory. It is used on a daily basis, a place where children play basketball and *caimaneras* (a simplified version of baseball that uses a stick for a bat and bottle caps for a ball). A hotdog cart and a small kiosk are testimonies of the plaza's daily pedestrian traffic. Festivities, religious celebrations, and concerts often take place in the renewed space.

Enlace Arquitectura's work with communities in informal settings focuses on defining the groundwork and

imagining how to re-signify open space as valuable. This is in contrast to other approaches that tend to build objects and structures. Through dialogues and workshops, professionals and neighbors have the opportunity to see their surroundings as opportunities; these conversations safeguard openness.

Extensive territories in Latin American cities are defined by informal urban development and the people who live there are often treated as secondary citizens. While it is true that these neighborhoods are in need of improvements in their services, amenities, and public spaces, recognizing these places as part of the city is the most important and less expensive investment. In addition to the physical intervention of building with communities, Enlace Arquitectura looks to create experiences for reflection through exhibitions, lectures, events, and publications that address the lingering negative stigma that people living in formal areas still maintain towards their neighbors living in informal areas. The idea is to build an acknowledgement of a cohesive city.

LOCATION: Chapellín, La Florida, Caracas, Venezuela / DATE: 2018 / SITE AREA: 258 sqm, 2,777 sf / ARCHITECTS: Elisa Silva, Miguel Salas, Eduardo Mouhtar, Sergio Dos Santos, Jeniree Calderon, Carol Arellano / COLLABORATORS: Roberto Patiño, Giorgina Cumarín, Oriana Medina, Jorge Somaca / ASSOCIATE: Caracas Mi Convive / CONSTRUCTION MANAGEMENT: Daniel Torrealba, Ruben Castellano CLIENT: Community of Chapellín / TEXT: Enlace Arquitectura / PHOTOS: Enlace Arquitectura

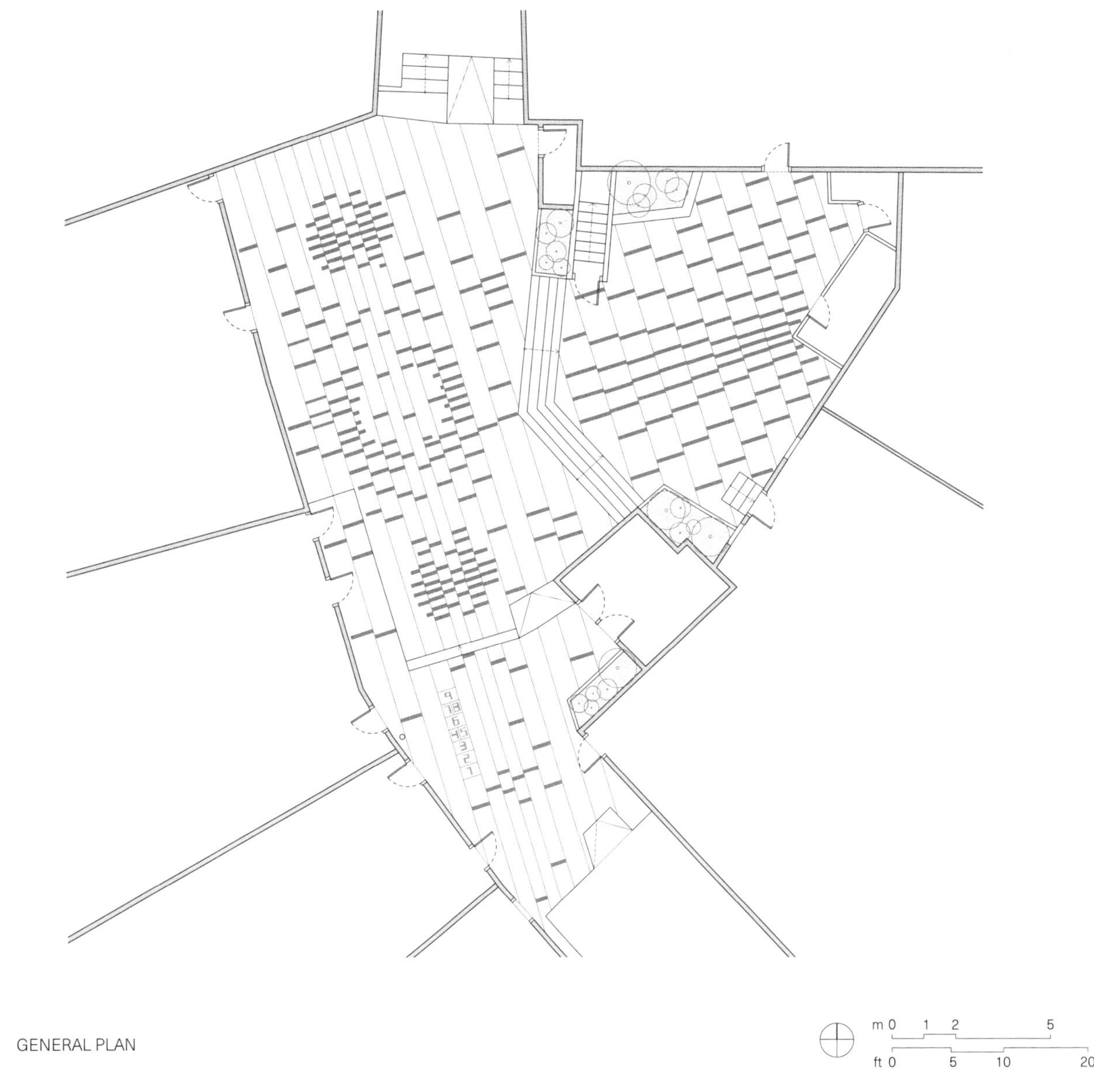

GENERAL PLAN

The project removed the existing decayed pavement, leveled the space to a single surface, and created a new pavement pattern with different concrete finishes. Steps and ramps mitigate the level changes and double as bleachers for people to sit on as they watch the children play.

—Enlace Arquitectura

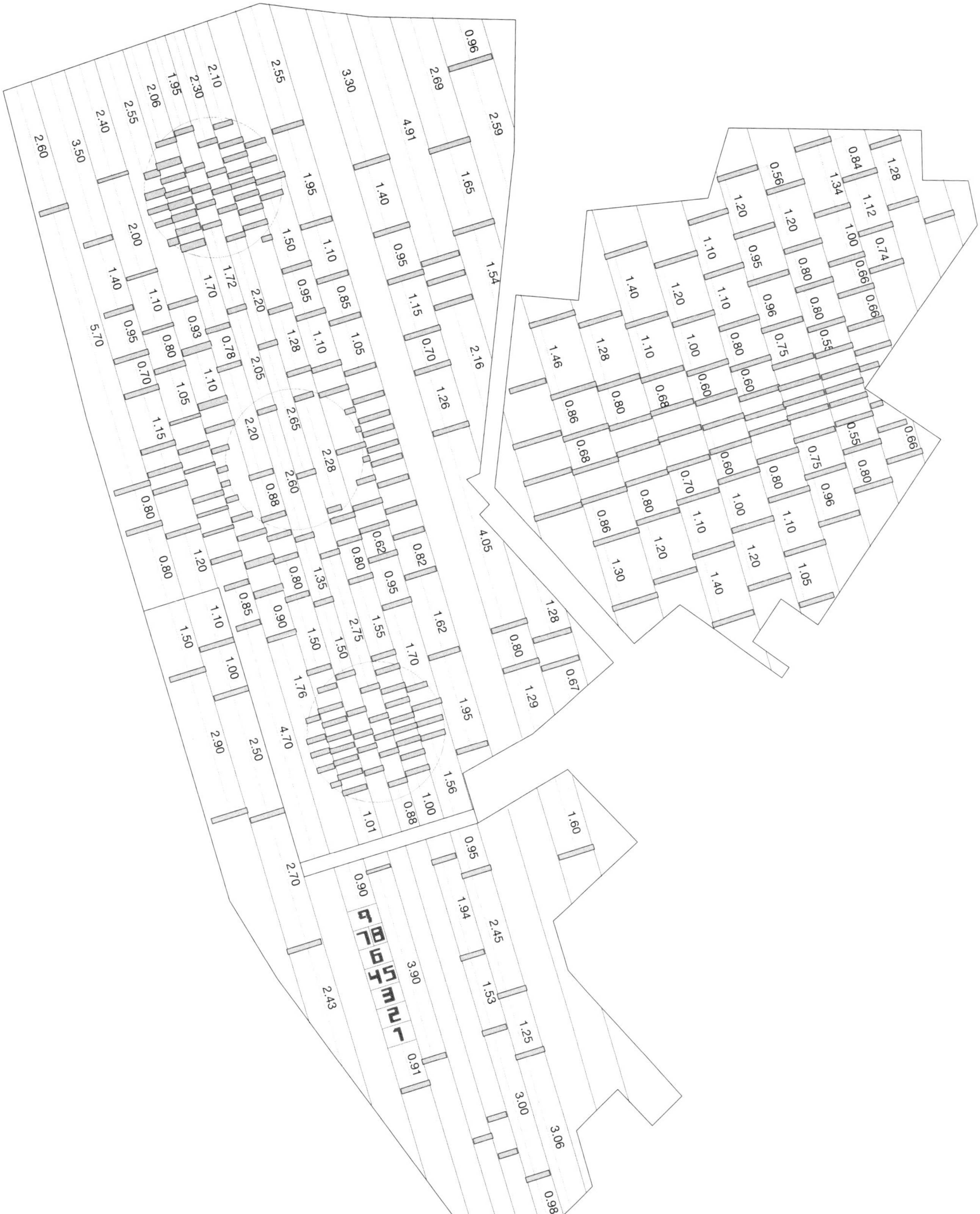
0.96
2.69
2.59
3.30
4.91
2.55
2.10
2.30
1.95
2.06
2.55
2.40
3.50
2.60
1.95
1.40
1.65
2.00
1.50
1.10
0.95
1.54
1.40
1.10
1.70
1.72
2.20
0.95
0.85
1.15
5.70
0.95
0.80
0.93
0.78
1.28
1.10
1.05
0.70
2.16
0.70
1.05
1.10
2.05
1.26
1.15
2.20
2.65
2.28
0.80
0.88
2.60
4.05
0.62
0.80
0.82
0.80
1.20
0.85
0.90
0.80
1.35
0.95
1.10
1.62
1.28
1.50
1.00
1.50
1.50
2.75
1.55
1.70
0.80
0.67
1.76
1.29
1.95
2.90
2.50
4.70
1.56
1.01
0.88
1.00
1.60
2.70
0.90
0.95
1.94
2.45
3.90
2.43
1.53
1.25
0.91
3.00
3.06
0.98
9
7
8
6
5
4
3
2
1
0.84
1.28
0.56
1.34
1.12
1.20
1.20
1.00
0.74
1.10
0.95
0.80
0.66
1.40
1.20
1.10
0.96
0.80
0.66
1.46
1.28
1.10
1.00
0.80
0.75
0.55
0.86
0.80
0.68
0.60
0.60
0.68
0.55
0.66
0.70
0.60
0.80
0.75
0.80
0.86
0.80
1.10
1.00
1.10
0.96
1.30
1.20
1.40
1.20
1.05

Performative Systems

This theme features program-driven strategies that incorporate climate and environmental indicators. These projects look to re-signify the increasing need for biodiversity in highly urbanized settings, where ecological performance becomes an asset for the city and its many publics. A speculative approach towards landscape enhances interactivity and responsiveness; designed ecosystems allow for the emergence of new relationships between complex programs and ecological infrastructures. Latent socio-spatial capacities emerge through a focus on public space and infrastructure; a new consciousness of everyday resources encourages us to rethink the idea of city as construct.

—Mercedes Peralta

Performative Systems

MANUEL GAUSA

I Operative Landscapes

The "Metapolis Dictionary of Advanced Architecture" provides a cryptic definition of the term Operative Landscapes:

"Landscapes, operative: See 'lands 1: land-links,' 'lands 2: land-arch,' and 'lands 3: lands-in-lands.'" (1)

The terms land-links, land-arch, and lands-in-lands defined a new territorial and urban multi-scalar conception of the landscape: hybrid, natural, and artificial, surpassing an attachment to the old notion of gardening architecture.

The notion of landscape as an adjective, with a voice operative, proposed a new vision for the traditional idea of the landscape, assimilating it to the concept of a system: an operative system was conceived not only as an eco-structure but also as an infra-structure, an intra-structure, a trans-structure, and a processing urban-territorial info-structure.

While the garden landscapes of the early 20th century were designed as pseudo-natures, the *Terrains Vagues* of the late 20th century were conceived of as latent voids or plots, announcing a vocation as city or urban places (more than Augian non-places). (2) By comparison, the new operational landscapes of the late 1990s and 2000s sought to formulate new hybrid devices (urban-natural, geographical-territorial, social-environmental, dilated and dense, topological and topographic, etc.).

This new vocation of the landscape as an urban-territorial active agent was born alongside the pioneering digital revolution, and an understanding of the dynamic and uncertain dendritic geometries and patterns that conformed the cities themselves, including their full-void-linked, occupational, interlaced, and diffused structures.

The landscape as a new operational device was not yet the old residue of an essential and substantive full but a new conjugative actor able to give a new type of elastic, cross-linkable, and infiltrated order, reconfigurable and recyclable, reactive or reversible, in a city that had manifested its growing and fractal condition as a complex system of systems, contingent and chaotic (in the most scientific sense of the term); multiple, heterogeneous, and undetermined.

The landscape, interpreted in an active and activist way, could become the real building of the new city: the structuring system of a possible multi-level order, more flexible and weighted, and no longer the extra possibility of the old planning.

The landscape was then an open order capable of meshing, relating, and redirecting the casual, irregular, and wild developments of current urban structures, generating more versatile—and non-imposing—relationship systems in resonance with the metropolitan dynamics themselves; their diffuse evolutions would tend to generate interstices, residual lands, border spaces, or large omission reserves operating in negative and in implicit and subjacent matrix networks.

This possibility, of course, had been favored in the transfer to a generation obsessed with the relationship between architecture and city (the city as a stable scenario, the result of the building) to another more sensitized by a new hybrid contract with a hybrid nature (artificial, functional, cross-bread, or wild, rather than domestic and bucolic).

Manuel Gausa *is an architect, critic, and author of several publications. Since 2017 he is the Chair of Urban Design as Full Professor at DAD-UNIGE, Università degli Studi of Genova, where from 2008 to 2014 he was Associate Professor of Design and from 2014 to 2017 Full Professor of Architecture and Landscape Design. Since 2015 he has served as the Director of the ADD (PhD Program in Architecture and Design). From 2012 to 2015 he was Dean of the IAAC (Institut d'Arquitectura Avançada de Catalunya, Barcelona). He is now Lead Senior Professor in Theory and Advanced Knowledge and member of the Scientific Board. He is also a Founding Member (1994) of Actar Publishers and Actar Arquitectura. In 2000 he was honored with the Médaille de l'Académie d'Architecture de France.*

New dynamics between architecture, urbanism, and landscape conformed a strange mixed vocabulary in which the action in the place would start from a new type of a-typologic contract between old taxonomic and divided categories, which no longer continued to create—as Le Corbusier signified—beautiful volumes in the light but rather ambiguous fields under the sky.

"Operational landscapes; relational enclaves capable of generating their own energy; informed fields within other reinforced fields."

II Performing Systems

At the beginning of the 21st century, the combination interaction-information is assumed as the great space-cultural revolution of our new era.

For many of the new actors implicated in these dilated processes of research, what was happening during the transfer of centuries was a change of paradigms: the pioneer explosion of a new operational logic, definitely innovative in its own idea of order, form, geometry, and materialization or organization.

A relational logic associated with the assumption of the complexity, the transversality, and the capacity for interaction between dynamic conditions and evolutionary processes are called to create intersections, encounters, hybridizations, mixtures, and interchanges, (3) not as mere compositional episodes but as adaptable and strategic-tactical systemic devices destined to combine global dynamics and local information simultaneously. (4)

If the strength of the iconic event-element continues to still be present in the urban cultures of the beginning of the century, then, in the most symptomatic research, this eventual condition would be combined with a clear vocation of multi-scalar transfers and interactions between places, times, programs, users, activities, and spaces aimed at generating relational environments rather than simple design objects. (5)

In the twenty years after the first pioneering insights of the 1990s, the first decades of the new century have experimented the exponential development of new technologies, opening up a new era of ever more ubiquitous and increased capabilities.

The emergence of the digital and informational universe of networked exchanges, parametric conceptions, digital and differential fabrications, environmental sensorizations, and online applications coincides with the appearance of new generations of actors more familiar with the premises of a new space-time-information logic. (6)

In the second decade of the 21st century, the first multi-scalar (and a-scalar) complex and transferring operations combined with a new type of more reactive and responsive, synergic, and empathic (natural and spontaneous) approach capable of combining not only "sense and sensitivity" but also sensorization and sensibilization. In the exploration of this new advanced logic of information and interaction, the pioneering architecture of simultaneity has given way to the architecture of instantaneity: an architecture of direct responses, of the moment rather than of the monument (the object-event) that seems to want to combine a new common logic (active and activist, optimized or simply positive) generated, on the whole, beyond the exceptional.

We are talking about an architecture correlated with a new sociocultural eco-mediation in which the natural and technological, sophisticated and spontaneous are conjugated, combining (beyond aesthetic prejudices or stylistic filters) the optimization of the simply necessary with a responsive and responsible vocation without linguistic claims or conventional aesthetic strains. Many of the most innovative and common architectures that occur today tend to emphasize the efficient management of information (in all senses, data, indicators, programs, conditions) and its immediate optimized formulation/resolution/translation in possible efficient and synthesized scenarios (more spontaneous or more sophisticated, more parametric or more filo-ethic).

The appearance of a new type of social-environmental sensitivity and direct action linked to an architecture of the immediate, the instantaneous, the impostergable (unpostponed) (7), connected to the *force de frappe* of the active and the activist, is marking the interest of new generations involved with this performative and collective sensibility (and the lesson of the Latin American and Hispanic experiences—from Madrid to Quito, from Caracas to Medellín—are, in this way, absolutely explicit and decisive). The dense set of interwined swimming pools and water activities in the Aquatic Center for the IX South-American Games in 2010, linked with similar experiences such as, Madrid Río, the loma (dunning Parque del Centro de Exposiciones y Convenciones, presented as a new Topo/Park civic roof above the semi-underground functional programs, the big reliefs of the re-natured terrains of the La Carlota Airport transformed into an open air active enclave are exploring new operational landscapes that start to be not only green spaces but also active surfaces. The bioclimatic prototype of the Edificio Jardín Hospedero y Nectarífero para Mariposas and its combination of artificial and natural sensitive and emotional feelings, the leisure deposed yellow light avatar-artifacts of the experiential circuits in The Garden of Forking Paths, and the interesting cultural park of Tiuna-El Fuerte designed and mediated by Alejandro Haiek in an old parking garage gained by the citizens and generated with recycled materials and containers as a civic and mixed-programs multilevel ground are evident demonstrations of these premises and these performing challenges and wills.

Boarding approaches generated by performative devices, strategic deployments or tactic guerrillas, without rhetoric or spectacular gestures but with a strong sense of commitment and of engagement, these dynamics provide solutions with imagination, fantasy, and intensity; proposals generated beyond typological standards or conventions.

The exploration of a new positive mediation (synergistic) to define our habitats, as well as a new sensitive interaction (empathic or eco-empathic) to deal with increasingly social complex scenarios, marks many of the essays produced today, in a time associated with global deficit situations related to conflicts and multiple threats linked to critical geopolitical (and geo-economic) oscillations. These are also, of course, related to climate changes that have devastating effects on the most vulnerable populations (risks, environmental problems, housing deficits, pollution, ghettoization, increase of poverty thresholds, etc.). (8)

New formulations in/with a milieu and in/with a reality not only distributed but also augmented in its own capacities of co(ll/nn)ective hyper-connection, and sensorization, are capable of combining social and technological conditions through more performing systems (and/or landscapes) oriented to favor an augmented enjoying of dynamic relations between citizens and environments, settlements and statements.

This direct, precise, dynamic, and instantaneous urban-answering (where the old systemic definition of the fixed element often gives way to a new epistemic condition of a real-time moment) continues to call, today, for the abilities of design but, above all, to the search for new shared informational/convivial processes, encouraging—incontestably—land-system-spaces definitely associated with the assumption of a new eco-medium and a new eco-mediation; spaces destined to exponentially expand this potential of exchange between conditions and situations, information(s), and solicitations, in the form of different formats, trajectories, and variable contexts.

The increasing development of new information technologies brings us exponentially closer to a reality recorded in a precise and immediate way, opening up an immense repertoire of possibilities in the field, of the combination between materiality, sociality, and spatiality and informa(tiona)lity from a mutual collaboration (in and with the urban landscapes) that is more efficient, responsible, convivial, and qualitative.

Hence, the concept of interaction (of a positive exchange between environment, society, and information) gains importance in relation to a more sustainable new development, not only as an ethical and socio-economic responsibility but also as a coherent consequence of these cultural-informational/relational revolution, today in course. (9)

(1) Gausa, Manuel; Guallart, Vicente; Muller, Willy; Morales, José; Porras, Fernando; and Soriano, Federico. "The Metapolis Dictionary of Advanced Architecture ," New York-Barcelona: Actar, 2003.

(2) With "Augian" we are using a neologism from the Non-Places of Marc Augé. See Augé, Marc. "Non-Places: An Introduction to Anthropology of Supermodernity," Paris: Le Seuil, 1992.

(3) Asher, François. "Métapoles ou l'Avenir des villes," Paris: Odile Jacob, 1995.

(4) Gausa, Manuel. "Open-Espacio-Tiempo-Información," New York-Barcelona: Actar, 2010.

(5) Ibid.

(6) Gausa, Manuel. City Sense: Territorializing Information, in "V.V.A.A.: City Sense, 4th Advanced Architecture Contest," Barcelona: Actar – IAAC, 2015.
With the title "Diálogos Impostergables" the central exhibition of the 2017 Biennial of Valparaíso was presented, curated by Felipe Vera and dedicated to a new social and resilient activism in Latin America. Within the event, conferences, debates, and round tables were held, including those moderated by Jeannette Sordi (Vulnerabilidad | Vulnerability) and Felipe Vera (Fundamentos | Fundaments). For further information see plataformaarquitectura.cl

(7) See the 15th Biennale di Architettura di Venezia, 2016, "Universes in Universe," curated by Alejandro Aravena.

(8) Baricco, Alessandro. "The Game," Torino: Einaudi, 2018.

Aquatic Center is a systemic landscape where water and users fluctuate between walled circulations. As architecture is taken as frame, it reinforces the idea of the role of people's movements in the shaping of the natural.

Aquatic Center

COLOMBIA

Luis Callejas (LCLA Office),

Edgar Mazo, Sebastián Mejía

In March 2008 an open international competition was held for a new aquatic center to host the IX Medellín South American Games. The competition brief asked for a compact building to host professional swimming competitions, synchronized swimming events, and two pools for training. Medellín is a tropical city with a consistently warm climate, making it possible to perform open air competitions year-around without the need of a contained atmosphere. The specific climatic conditions of Medellín gave us the idea to suggest a park-like facility rather than an enclosed building. The site, located on the west side of the city, was formerly a go-cart track. It is framed by the city's striking geography.

Our winning proposal responded with a fully open-air swimming complex for professional and recreational aquatic sports that can act as a public aquatic park when professional competitions are not taking place. The project responded to the complexities of the brief.

The new aquatic center's competition brief asked to meet the needs of future competitions as well as to consider its availability as a new teaching facility and public pool. In response, the layout is articulated by a garden system through which the four pools are connected. A flooded landscape planted with species typical of tropical wetlands separates private and public spaces that otherwise would have ended up as vertical partitions.

The competition brief required a complex system of bathrooms and changing rooms for swimmers and the public. All these areas are placed beneath the aquatic gardens. A set of below-ground courtyards provide natural light as well as a meeting space and warm-up area for competitors. This piece of basement-level architecture almost resembles a piece of land art, its labyrinthine pathways and architecture look like furrows in the Earth. The only construction that rises above the gardens is the synchronized swimming pool. Submerged windows face the main open-air circulation area and, from the street, passersby can peek in at the synchronized swimmers. Rather than watching the competition in a cube of water, spectators are positioned to look out over an aquatic landscape.

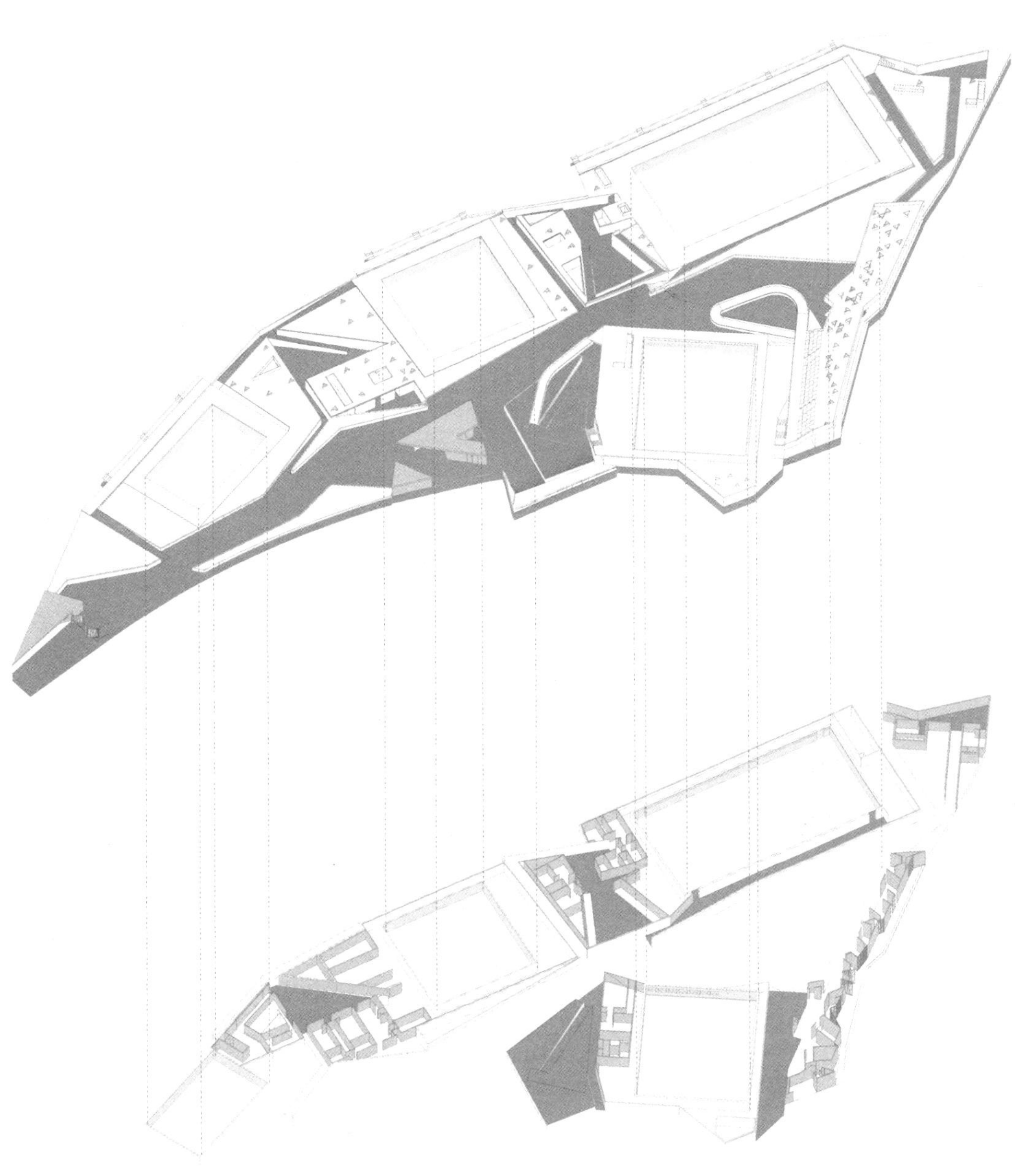

LOCATION: Medellín, Colombia / PROJECT DATE: 2008 / FINAL DATE: 2010 / AREA: 16,000 sqm, 172,222,57 sf / DESIGN: Luis Callejas (LCLA Office), Edgar Mazo, Sebastián Mejía / COMPETITION TEAM: Juanita González, Eliana Beltrán, Sebastián Betancur, Andrés Zapata, Clara Arango, Adriana Tamayo / PROJECT TEAM: Farid Maya, Sebastián Monsalve, Luis Tobón, Iván Forgionni, Juan Sebastián Pérez, Andrés Zapata, Sebastián Serna, Juan Esteban Gómez, Érica Martínez, Aura Cuartas / LANDSCAPE DESIGN: Luis Callejas, Edgar Mazo, Sebastián Mejía, Andrés Ospina / CONSULTANTS: Jorge Aristizabal, structural engineering / CLIENT: Medellín Mayor's Office, Inder, Coldeportes TEXT: Design Team / PHOTOS: Luis Callejas, Juan E. Gómez (p. 94)

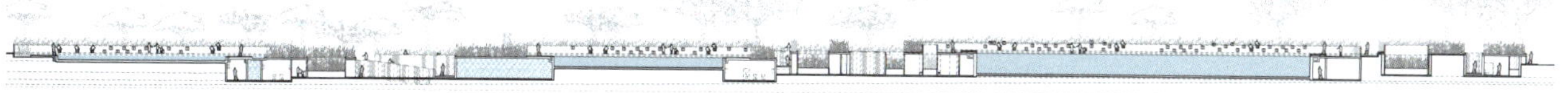

SECTION

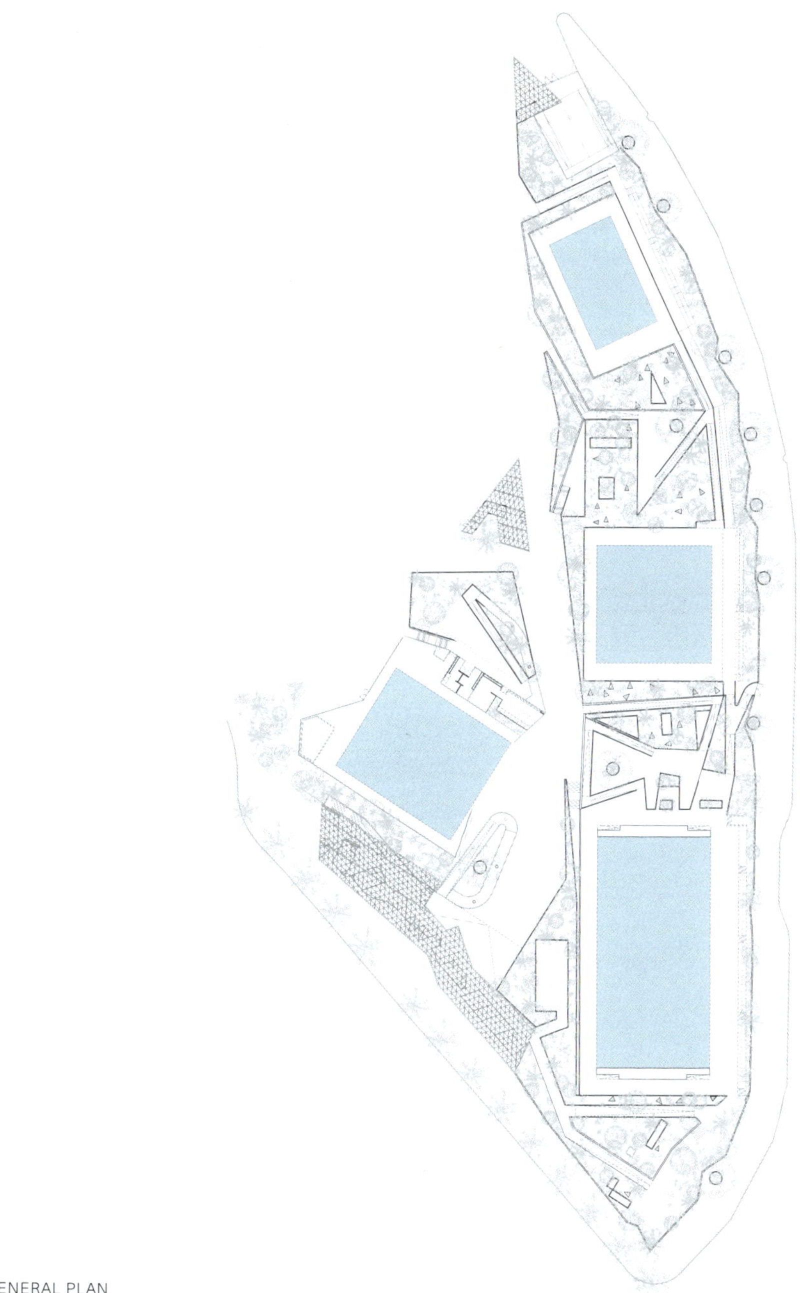

GENERAL PLAN

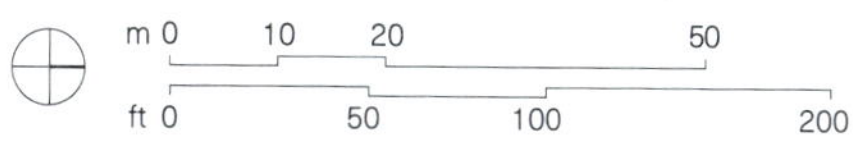

This park on top of a topographic building articulates a continuity between two other adjoining urban parks. New materials are tested and biological urban dynamics are redesigned.

Parque del Centro de Exposiciones y Convenciones

ARGENTINA

Bulla

"The only possibility of being visible is to be able to exaggerate." –Martín Rein Cano

Bulla is a hybrid organization that combines architecture, landscape, urban planning, and nature. It analyzes the global environmental context in order to translate it into local culture, taking up the traditions of the city's historical landscape designers, its public space, activism, explores research as well as new social phenomena. Bulla engages in a tactic of interruption in the established urban, political, and environmental scene of Buenos Aires. It is a practice of rupture, kinetics, and visibility. Rupture generates a change of an era and generation; kinetics implies a new process of building disciplinary certainties through constant exploration and experimentation; and visibility is the act of exaggerating the invisible and evading the cultural camouflage of landscape.

This new disciplinary agenda blends perspectives in the natural sciences with urban planning strategies and project techniques from South American cities. Cities and nations developed on a mosaic of landscapes that were neglected/denied/destroyed by modern culture. From the re-exploration of large regional biomes to endemic botany, and from the formation of great landscape models to the local water cycle, Bulla understands the city and public space as an invitation to experiment in the present, inviting the incorporation of new interdisciplinary knowledge and languages. The organization has developed series of episodes as projects that engage questions of social appropriation, cultural construction, and ecological reconnection. The Parque del Centro de Exposiciones y Convenciones (CEC) was one of those first trials, conducted in 2012.

The CEC, designed together with Edgardo Minond and his team, explores, from an urban point of view, the possibility of building a new park-hub from old nature. It is a park within other parks, an unprecedented condition for the city. It is also a new botanical ideology that redefines the aesthetics of public space as well as a model that inaugurates an eco-systemic era for the public parks of Buenos Aires. It calls for a revision of gardening and space management techniques over time.

The Reserve Territory (*escape*, 2017) (1) questions those vestiges and the potentials of the terrestrial ecosystem: natural reserves, urban parks, baldío squares, and botanical tests. The CEC figures as a type of trial where new materials are tested and biological urban dynamics are redesigned.

These experiences are a machinery of intellectual and material production, both collective and collaborative. They represent an ability to design and build devices and material, biotic, and abiotic experiences that re-program and challenge the link between nature and humans. They are a future ideology of a hybrid and artificial nature with biologically-active functions that improve the quality of urban life. They rethink communities as ecological and social units, as new models for living collaboratively. And finally, they also rethink the infrastructures and economies associated with ecoregions and phytogeography, the urban planning in the territory, and the understanding of ecology as a technology.

(1) *escape* is a cycle of conferences organized by Bulla. It is based on the relationship between the Argentinian territory and its culture, which seeks to enrich the relationship between different disciplines and the landscape.

LOCATION: Buenos Aires, Argentina / DATE: 2014-2017 / SITE AREA: 18,000 sqm, 193,750.39 sf / LANDSCAPE PROJECT: Bulla (Ana García Ricci, Ignacio Fleurquin, Lucía Ardissone, Alejandra Yamasato, Pablo Rubio) / LANDSCAPE CONSULTANT: Gabriel Burgueño ARCHITECTURE PROJECT: Edgardo Minond, architect / ARCHITECTURE TEAM: Mariano Albornoz, Margarita María Descole, Laura di Chello, Roberto Alejandro Morita, architects, Maximiliano Manuel Rodríguez, Lucía Galeano, Juan Manuel Galleano, Daniel Nazareno de Souza, Manuel Luis Mosquera, Angela Pérez Loret / TEXT: Bulla / PHOTOS: Fernando Schapochnik

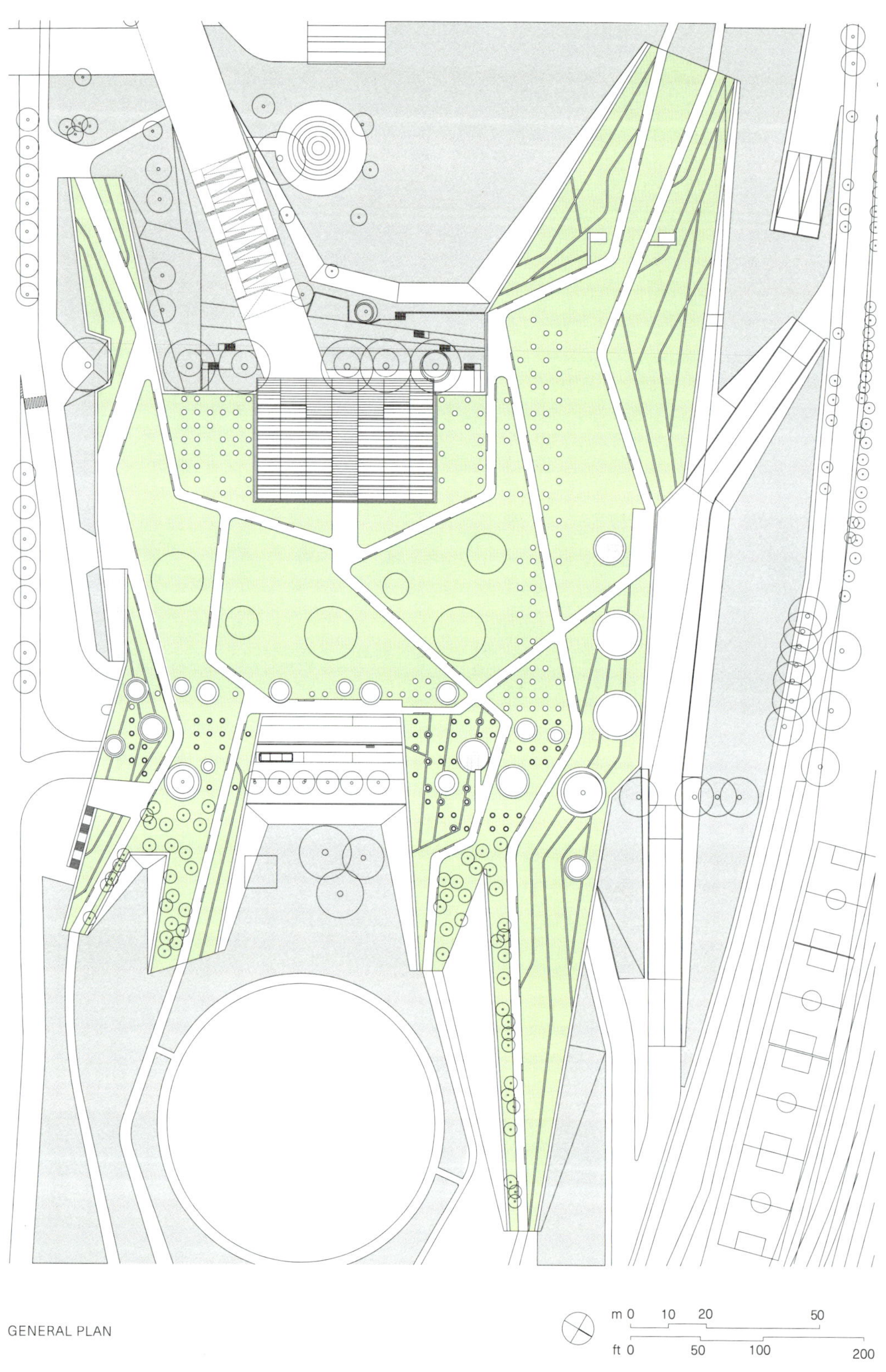

GENERAL PLAN

Two opposite urban situations are linked through the use of bridges that are not looking for uniformity but rather a succession of smaller areas to linger. The project achieves a balance between systematic continuity and individual programmatic uses.

Parque Botánico Río Medellín

COLOMBIA

Juan David Hoyos,
Sebastián Monsalve

This project arose from a need to improve the infrastructure of a national highway that runs through the city and is parallel to the river. The city's administration saw the project as an opportunity to recover the urban waterfront.

In the 1950s, the city government rectified and canalized Medellín's river to eliminate flood areas and establish a national mobility corridor along its banks. This caused the city to divide in two, with 1.2 million people living on the east side of the river and another 1.2 million on the west side. The built connections between the two sides are designed exclusively for automobile traffic. The aim of the competition was to develop transversal pathways using quality public spaces that could recover the river's significance for its citizens, generating use beyond its function as a mobility corridor. It also aimed to acknowledge the river's natural and environmental importance.

The Parque Botánico Río Medellín promotes moving from urban sprawl towards a densification of the urban core, creating high-value areas that support the Land Ordinance Plan (POT) and its focus on a more sustainable development.

The project serves as a structural response to the biotic network of the city of Medellín. It proposes the river as a structuring axis and takes advantage of the natural hierarchy of the riverbed to create a botanical park that articulates the natural systems of the city in a larger environmental circuit within the territory.

Through its design and program, the park aims to develop environmental awareness while preserving and reintroducing native species to communicate with surrounding biotic networks. Every pathway, boulevard, and open space is associated with a specific species, bringing together activities, people, and nature. Isolated green spaces surrounding the project and related to the river and its creeks are categorized, reused, and reconnected to the biotic corridor.

The project rehabilitates creeks by promoting the recovery and protection of all small waterways that flow into the river and reintegrating them into the main biotic network. It also recycles underused structures along the river by giving them new uses.

The Parque Botánico Río Medellín strengthens the river as a biotic, active, and dynamic corridor. It shifts the landscape design from ornamental and individualized species to native flora, augmenting interchange and its transformative capacity and enhancing urban biodiversity. Using succession models of species over time, it generates greater cohesion among the proposed associations and creates a pathway to a more complex ecosystem.

LOCATION: Medellín, Colombia / DATE: 2014-2016 / SITE AREA: 17 km / PROJECT: Juan David Hoyos, Sebastián Monsalve, architects LANDSCAPE DESIGN: Nicolás Hermelín / TEAM: Osman Marín, Luis Alejandro Jiménez, Juan Diego Martínez, María Clara Trujillo, Alejandro Vargas, David Castañeda, David Mesa, Carolina Zuluaga, Daniel Zuluaga, Sara París, Daniel Beltrán, Daniel Felipe Zuluaga, Alejandro López, Andrés Velásquez, Juan Camilo Solís, Melissa Ortega, Andrés Santiago Fajardo, Viviana Velásquez Amaya, David Hernández del Valle, Carolina Vélez, Laura Elena Zuluaga, Daniel Peláez, Juan Pablo Martínez, María Camila Henao, Lukas Serna, Diana Herrera, Daniel González, Andrea Maruri, Marly Duque, María Paula Rico, Sebastián González Bolívar / CONSULTANTS: Consorcio EDL, engineering design; Consorcio Integral – Interdiseños, construction management / CLIENT: Medellín Government / TEXT: Juan David Hoyos, Sebastián Monsalve / PHOTOS: Juan Sebastián Saldarriaga (p. 103), Alejandro Arango (p. 104 above), Sebastián González Bolívar (p. 104 below)

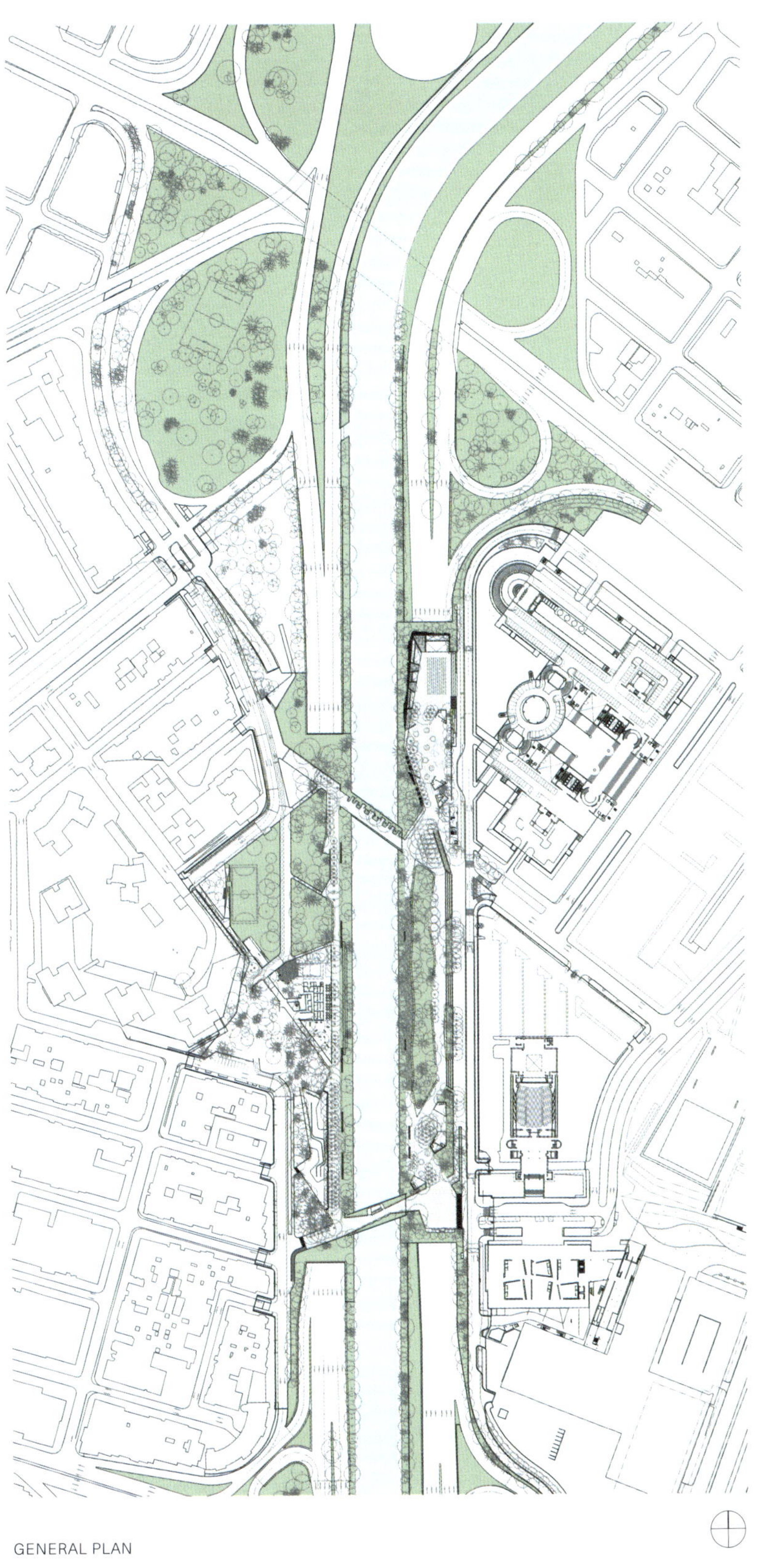

GENERAL PLAN

The existing site dynamics are strengthened through the creation of an open space at the underground level of the metro and the parking zone. The new cultural and commercial programs resonate with the uses of this public space.

Plaza Houssay

ARGENTINA

RDR Arquitectos

We are interested in the city as a scenario of efficient human development with low environmental impact. In Latin America, during the last few years, there has been a shift from the idea of the suburban city to the compact, medium-density city that can invest more heavily in its infrastructure, transportation, and public spaces. One definition of the city that is of interest to us is the city as a living organism and, accordingly, we consider our tasks to be those of general practitioners, turning our attention to the problem, working with urban planners, landscape architects, officials, developers, etc.

Plaza Houssay was a project that had the potential to articulate these reflections. The idea that guided the competition was a strong basis for action as it already contained criterion for reducing the number of parking lots in central areas and incorporating programs that encourage the use of the square at night. In most of our architectural works, we explore both urban and landscape conditions. We deal with them simultaneously—in other words, as they are lived. Recently, in our office in Buenos Aires, we have been reflecting on the city's parks, their constant evolution, the reconfiguration of their borders, and their defective equipment.

We recently handed in a project for the lower Mitre Viaduct contest. This project was done more on the basis of a circumstantial need to occupy the space rather than with a particular vision for the city. Our presentation focused on establishing the urban priorities that we consider essential so as not to lose the opportunity that the raising of the railway tracks offered (the relevance of the viaduct and its urban externalities were not a subject of debate and consensual planning).

In Plaza Houssay, where we worked with Grupo Landscape, the challenge was to integrate all of the equipment required by the competition specifications without losing a single square meter of qualified public space. At the same time, this made it possible to generate more dynamic uses and connections that animate the square.

One of the characteristics of urban planning in Argentina in recent times is that many works do not arise from a process of consensual and logical planning. Instead, they are traversed by many factors that sometimes completely sterilize the built places. The challenge is to redirect these processes towards more rigorous, realistic, and consensual planning. In order to define the projects in our practice, we are attentive to the future potential of the areas in which we intervene. It becomes, in this way, an enterprise of project and planning.

LOCATION: Buenos Aires, Argentina / DATE: 2017 (competition), 2019 (construction) / BUILT AREA: 46,000 sqm, 495,139.87 sf / CLIENT: LAMP Investments / STATUS: Built / DESIGN TEAM: Ignacio Dahl Rocha, Bruno Emmer, Facundo Morando, architects / COLLABORATORS: Rodrigo Muro, Roberto Lombardi, Sofía Vivacqua, Martina de Barba, Clara Carrera, Juan Benítez, Facundo Burgos, Matías Brun, Tomás Pérez Amenta, Nicolás Adrian, Lucía Iglesias, architects / CONSULTANTS: Sebastián Berdichevsky, Structural Engineering, Julio Argentino Blasco Diez, Thermomechanical Engineering, Marcelo Alignani, José Portela, Electrical Installation, Verónica Gilotau, Lighting LANDSCAPE: Grupo Landscape / TEXT: RDR Arquitectos / PHOTOS: Javier Agustín Rojas

GENERAL PLAN

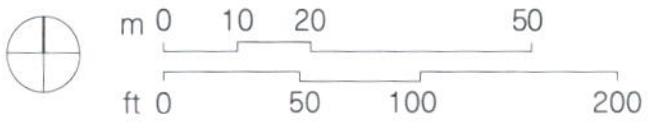

m 0 10 20 50
ft 0 50 100 200

BUS

As the picturesque scene is inverted and traversed, the theatricality of landscape becomes lived in and the cityscape is the abstraction in the distance.

The Garden of Forking Paths

CHILE

Beals Lyon Arquitectos

One of the first projects we completed since formally beginning our practice was The Garden of the Forking Paths. It was also the first time we approached landscape and architecture without making a distinction between them, being able to break a dialectic condition between nature and the built environment.

The brief for this competition requested a pavilion in a park. However, our project was not about creating a building in green surroundings, but rather about asking how we could become a part of the park. We wanted to intensify the experience of the place in order to reveal its qualities through a new series of situations of exploration and discovery.

When we think about buildings in a park, we can make a fundamental distinction. On the one hand, we have pavilions, which are usually seen as isolated forms or iconic shapes read against the landscape, built to be perceived mostly visually from the outside. On the other hand, we have typologies like the enclosed garden, the grotto, and the labyrinth which are conceived from within, demanding a certain exploration in order to understand and experience them. They have an ambiguous nature: they are simultaneously natural and artificial, interior and exterior, public and intimate. We wanted to be part of this second group.

Since then, we have considered every project, no matter its scale or context, not as an isolated object but instead with the conviction that it must be heavily related to the site where it is located. By doing so, we can also transform the perception and experience of the landscape where we operate, moving beyond the actual boundaries of the site. We think of landscape and architecture as one continuous entity or, at least, different scales of the same problem.

When we approach the subject of landscape, we think about it dynamically. That is, we consider it both in terms of its continuously-evolving qualities and also in terms of how we perceive landscape through the experience of motion, which implies situations of exploration and discovery, of quietness and surprise.

In a context where it is already hard to differentiate between the natural and the artificial world, where urban sprawl is taking

over what was previously regarded as natural surroundings and nature is infiltrating our cities, we cannot help but understand landscape as the urbanism of our era. Boundaries between the natural and artificial are becoming blurred, and it is becoming harder to differentiate one from the other.

We do not trust in excessive specialization in our discipline: landscape, urbanism, infrastructure, architecture, everything is related and cannot be isolated. We must therefore consider the full scope of every project, understanding that each intervention is a part of a broader living organism, a landscape, where changing a part of it will affect the whole body.

LOCATION: Parque Araucano, Santiago, Chile / DATE: 2013 / SITE AREA: 1,500 sqm, 16,145.87 sf / ORIGIN: Winning Proposal for the YAP-CONSTRUCTO 2012/13, MoMA PS1 Young Architects Program / PROJECT: Alejandro Beals, Loreto Lyon, architects / COLLABORATORS: Claudio Viñuela, Francisca Becerra / CONSTRUCTION: Juan Candia / PHOTOS: Cristóbal Palma

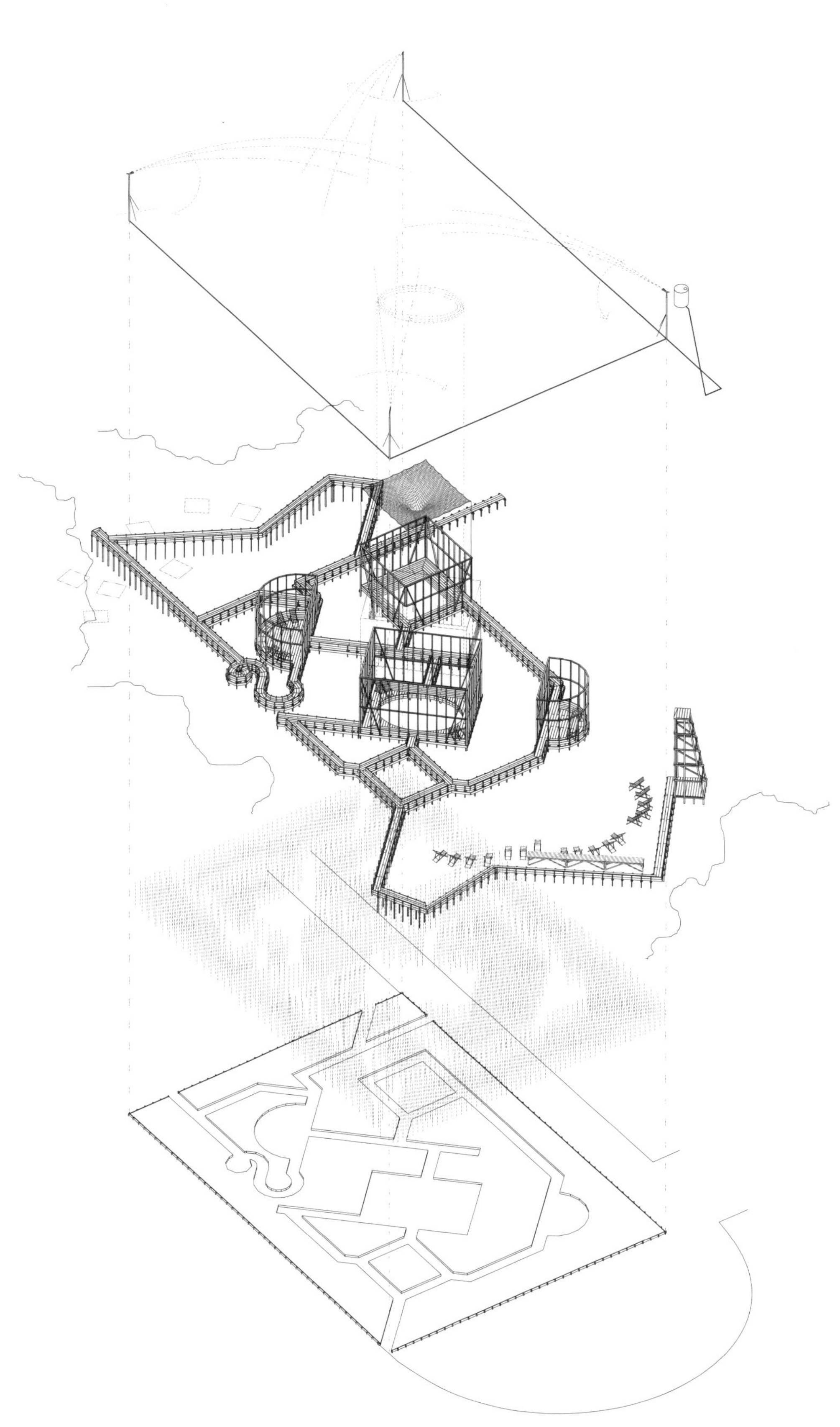

EXPLODED AXONOMETRIC

THE POND

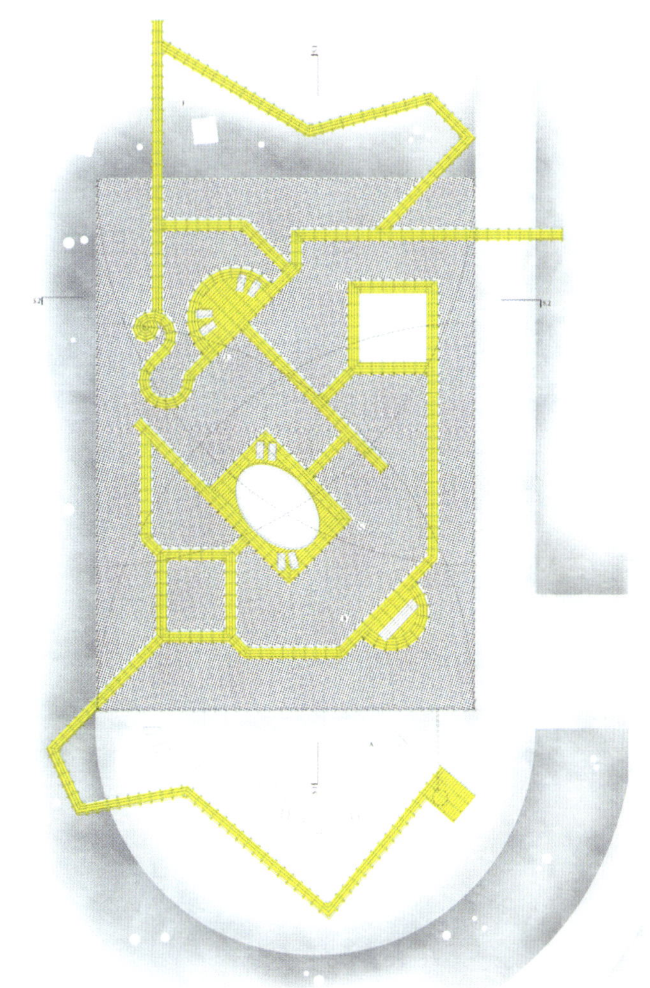

GROUND PLAN

THE MUSIC ROOM

Revealed Protocols

Systemic approaches are not simply concerned with complexity, forms of organization, and scheme or method consistency. Revealed Protocols interrogates various procedural modes of landscape that suggest new possibilities for urbanism. Rejecting the scenic and the picturesque, these projects instead engage with geographical, social, and economic conditions and their attendant cultural and environmental ramifications. Experimental or diagrammatic visual vocabularies highlight the need for less orthodox means of representation.

Systemic Landscapes

JOSÉ ALFREDO RAMÍREZ

Landscape as a profession has barely taken off in Latin America, despite nature being one of the most salient and diverse features of the region. The apparent separation between cities and their hinterlands right from the foundations of their history has played an important role. Since the colonization period in the 16th and 17th centuries, a stark divide between human settlements and nature was established, irrespective of the dependence of the former on the latter. One of the key factors in generating this division was the Law of the Indies (1), a document that instituted design rules for the ordered layout of new settlements. This document created modern generic models that structured all historic centers designed in Latin America. The Law of the Indies established a basic structure: a main square around which a regular and expanded grid extended outward. Nearly a thousand towns and cities eventually shared these features across the vast continent. Regardless of the fact that these urban structures adjusted, adapted, and were modified in relation to local geographical, socio-economic, and political contexts in various and messy ways, they all shared a vision: the control of nature and, thus, of local communities. These rational urban centers were separated from the vast hinterlands and its resources in order to fuel the power of the metropolises and cities on which they center.

One of the clearest examples of this mentality is Mexico City. The entire history of that metropolis reflects a battle to control nature, an image of nature beneficial to certain social groups. For various and complicated reasons, mainly economic and political, the powerful elite authorities encouraged the elimination of the system of lakes on which the city was founded (2). The nature of these lakes was constantly fluctuating in accordance with rainy and dry seasons; their shifting rich soils and biomass shaped local customs and communities for centuries. The new era prioritized a mentality that advanced clearly-demarcated property boundaries to protect newly colonized territories, partly instrumentalizing local knowledge (3); it was a format that continued throughout the city's evolution and expansion. Control over these territories included the seasonal lake cycles, which disappeared, re-emerging today in the city's natural disasters: flooding and subsidence. Today, Mexico City still struggles to control and separate itself from nature—a problem visible in its increasingly failing infrastructures that ignore former landscapes and alternative indigenous relationships between nature and society. What is more, the city has now expanded its control and extraction of natural resources beyond its geographical location. Former rivers, lakes and wetlands have given way to streets, buildings, highways, and colossal water infrastructure supply and sewage systems in a continuous thirst to define and fix the boundaries between city and nature.

The Landscape as Urbanism conferences around Latin America have expanded the notion of landscape from the perspective of design, helping to stir debates about our visions of nature and what they mean for the region. These debates have foregrounded the possibility that landscapes might become part of a new mentality towards urban environments, one that surpasses the green washing and superficial landscape validations found in conventional urban development. Even though the Landscape as Urbanism conferences originated in a Western context that is geographically and historically distanced from Latin American environments, they have been crucial in bringing forward a fundamental subject for the region. Several design precedents (in the form of built and design projects in the region) (4) demonstrate landscape's critical capacity of to generate a shift in mentalities.

José Alfredo Ramírez *is an architect, director of Groundlab, and Co-Director of the Landscape Urbanism Post Graduate Programme at the Architectural Association in London. Ramírez leads research projects that investigate the agency of design within Earth systems and the production of territorial projects to face climate change and planetary urbanization. He has led the development of large-scale projects at the junction of architecture, landscape, and urbanism in a variety of contexts such as China, Mexico, Spain, Russia, Chile, and the UK, among others. Ramírez is a dual Mexican and British citizen and he regularly publish essays. He gives lectures on the topics of design, landscape, and urbanism.*

Within this historical and geographical context, Landscape as Urbanism put forward landscape-oriented models that will bring systemic changes to urbanization processes in Latin America. The imposing generic rules established by the Laws of the Indies ignored historical or geographical genealogies for the sake of economic and efficient infrastructures that facilitated settlement, colonization, and specific power relations. Instead, critical landscape-oriented models entail a complete rethinking of the dynamics of urbanization, a process that James Bridle called (in technological terms) "systemic literacy" (5). Systemic literacy is the capacity not only to understand how things (urban landscapes, in our case) work or perform, but also how they came to be (historically and geographically) and how they continue to work today, even if the tightly interwoven resources and relations they draw from (other landscapes and territories) are hidden and invisible to us.

A systemic literacy of urban landscapes will help us, first, to think about the socio-economic conditions, geographical and environmental features, climatic and atmospheric aspects, cultural and symbolic practices, as well as the territories, and the material and labor that they have historically been dependent on. It would include the political technologies and laws through which these visions are put forward, such as cartographic practices or economic policies. Taken together, it will represent a process we refer to as Territorial Praxis (6). Second, using these territorial lenses will help us design landscapes and think about their implementation in urban prototypes, addressing larger complex and overarching urban and landscape systems. This is a process seen, explored, and implemented in various projects presented in Landscape as Urbanism conferences and in this issue of NESS.docs. From the territorial lens, urban prototypes are conceived as intrinsically dependent on their context; they are openly aware of the territories and landscapes, the power relationships and urban systems, in a broad sense, on which they depend. Urban prototypes prioritize process over form, critical thinking over technological solutionism, and can negotiate and influence bottom-up approaches (community-led projects) with top-down regulations (policy design).

Rather than a focus on the production of specific products with a final fixed image and delivery date, landscape urbanism requires us to rethink landscape as a way to generate systemic literacy within the profession. Beyond the design of single buildings or examples of urban and landscape design, landscape urbanism can expand the agency of design to produce spatial policies, organizational models, innovative regulatory plans, or visual decision-making tools. In short, it represents seeing landscape design (projects and policies) and their implementation as urban prototypes from a territorial praxis as key elements in the re-thinking of the relationship between nature and society in Latin America.

(1) Laws of the Indies, available at en.wikipedia.org/wiki/Laws_of_the_Indies.

(2) Candiani, Vera S. "Dreaming of Dry Land: Environmental Transformation in Colonial Mexico Cit," Stanford University Press, 2014.

(3) Ibid.

(4) See projects shown in this –NESS.docs issue.

(5) Bridle, James. "New Dark Age: Technology and the End of the Future," Verso, 2018.

(6) Olóriz Sanjuán, Clara. "Landscape as Territory," Actar, 2019.

Some Kind of Nature

CIRO NAJLE

Some kind of nature
Some kind of soul
Some kind of mixture
Some kind of goal
Some kind of majesty
Some chemical load (1)

Protocols are sets of stabilized dynamic relationships between systems operating at multifarious levels that when assembled in a model—strict, determinable, rational, technical—abstract the vicissitudes of a phenomenon according to an internally consistent set of rules, turning its indeterminacy upside down and constructing a more or less generic, more or less peculiar, form of architecture, before architecture. By means of the regulation of these relationships, protocols enable the control and connection between disparate and often mutually irreducible forms of computation in a single net, permitting the transference of information and governing the syntax and the synchronization of their communication. However extensive, rather than aggregating relationships ad infinitum, this net is finite and confined, even if this confinement relies on diffuse and precarious limits. As a consequence, its construction involves not just the cumulative incorporation of restrictions but also their inherently conscious organization within a consistent machine of formation with hierarchies of dependence and interdependence. Such a machine must be understood—rather than as a flexible, accommodating, instrumental, and formless set—as having, or progressively acquiring, a form by its own right, an active kind of form. The form of a protocolar machine is articulated by a model, a singular piece of denatured nature that operates as a pre-architecture, that stands somewhere after the loss of the alleged naturalness of the processes contained and before their idealization in an essence, a truth, or a coherent, autonomous logic; that is, before the crystallization of its rules in an invariable format or a hard operative system. Assembled and coalesced within a consistent model of this kind, protocols sharpen otherwise disaggregated and unpredictable processes into deliberate and determinable procedures and, by means of the form in which they are assembled, constitute what can be regarded as an etiquette. Far from naturalistic truths, etiquettes are customary codes that surpass the simplistic notion of the behavior they seem to incarnate because they assume the intrinsic artificiality and artistic character of their construct, building up a whole aesthetic system—a decorum—out of the awareness of its form, be this awareness explicitly stipulated or implicitly embedded within it. The modalities of these models—the co-dependent intertwinement of sets of variables in clusters and other minor complexes, as well as their regimes of difference, the ranges of variability, thresholds, liminal conditions, and qualitative leaps they involve—assemble together along a series of guidelines and structures that constitute their form, which not only holds together protocols into a complex system of systems but, furthermore, organizes them and puts them in resonance with one another, aesthetizing their arrangement along the lines of a taste or a sense and feeding them back with mandates, commands, authorizations, permissions, and restrictions coming from a higher—and intensely arbitrary—level that commands them from the top while being built from the bottom. Radically opposite to any essence, this arrangement involves the construction of an inherently insubstantial—yet not merely trivial—apparatus that, while standing on its own feet, is transient and evanescent. If the stratified formal structures of architecture that systematize and broadcast themselves

Ciro Najle *is an architect (honors) from the Universidad de Buenos Aires and Master of Advanced Architectural Design (honors) from Columbia University. Ciro Najle is Dean and Professor of the Escuela de Arquitectura y Estudios Urbanos at the Universidad Torcuato Di Tella in Buenos Aires. He was the Diploma Unit Master and Director of the Landscape Urbanism Graduate Program at the Architectural Association and Visiting Professor at Harvard GSD, Cornell, Columbia, the Berlage Institute, and the Universidad de Buenos Aires. Director of the General Design Bureau in Buenos Aires, and previously of Mlab and of MID, and the winner of the Young Architect of the Year Second Prize in London, his work has been widely published in international media. He is author of the following books "The Generic Sublime" (Actar / Harvard GSD), "Suprarural" (Actar), with Lluís Ortega, and "Landscape Urbanism, A Manual for the Machinic Landscape" (AA), with Mohsen Mostafavi, and editor of "Superdigitalismos" (CPAU). His publications include writings in Quaderns, 2G, Space, Oris, Praxis, Harvard Design Magazine, UR, i+t, Egg, and Summa+, the interview series Out of Time (Plot), and the introductions to the 2G Monographs on FOA and MGM (GG).*

as canons, archetypes, types, and traditions have historically claimed for a meta-historical status that classifies material organizations according to a rigid referential system that assures the permanence and universality of its objects and the truthfulness and meta-discursiveness of their values, protocols operate as the medium and the vehicle of ever-incomplete yet singular models of generation of new forms of intelligence—unstable canons, playful archetypes, differentiated types, and willfully built traditions. They incarnate and keep in motion the recurring self-learning of the discipline and the progressive self-renewal of the practice of architecture. Far beyond simulating the natural through operative systems driven by production, the self-standing condition of an architectural model lies in the peculiar form of its construction and is directed not just to the assurance of their relevance and productivity but to the sharpening and endurance of the form of its protocolar manifold, which is sustained with poignancy, consistency, and ability to exert influence. Consequently, with this artificiality, along the lines of its peculiarity, and far from the operative optimization of processes that takes place by means of its regulation, the sheer form of this rule apparatus, the escalating excess of these rules, its passionate self-fueling drive, and the chronically-insufficient artificiality of its tendency to configure a fully formed etiquette turn a model into a self-superseding construct that, on the one hand, abstracts its sources and provides them with a self-standing form, and on the other transcends its premises and overwhelms this very form. Paradoxically, the protocols assembled in a model trigger this trend from within, and, instead of necessarily consolidating established mechanisms, they are capable of unleashing radical forms of freedom that bypass any dependence on goodness, exceed frames of correctness, overcome the will to optimization, transform parameters of efficiency, transmute values, and redefine the notion of what is commonly regarded as normal, configuring a new horizon of what the discipline can become. Through sheer excess, the conventions and routines directed towards the stabilization, control, and prediction of processes become in this way volatile and erratic, and they do so by their own means and through their own mechanisms of order. When such uncanny, improbable unfolding happens, the initially denaturalized set builds up for itself a new kind of nature—one operating at a second, artificial level—that projects a model onto the world to transform it according to the artificially wild form of its rules. This new kind, by definition unnatural, involves an entirely new form of otherness.

(1) Albarn, Damon; Hewlett, Jamie; and Reed, Lou. "Some Kind of Nature," Gorillaz in Plastic Beach. Parlophone Records Limited. Recorded June 2008/November 2009. Released March 2010.

Through the study of many disputed island territories, cataloguing becomes a method for interpreting geographical problems. The same island is transformed through a drawing action, and a system is built through fragments, glimpses of patterns, varied formations.

Pelagic Alphabet

VARIOUS LOCATIONS

LCLA Office

Forty oceanic islands are subject to different forms of territorial claims. Some have been contested for centuries, while others behave as enclaves for future extraction sites in open oceans.

The project began by looking at specific conflicts happening in the Caribbean, specifically the ongoing dispute between Nicaragua and Colombia for the Roncador and Quitasueño cays. From this starting point the project reveals how territorial disputes are often addressed by the international courts through the study of hidden underwater topography.

As attention is usually focused on buildings and structures, the ceramic objects intensify the topographic features that could define a different division of land in these islands. Ultimately, the project attempts to unravel sovereignty as a material condition driven by the objectification of the ground.

While these handmade ceramic models of islands are accurate in plan projection, elevations are deformed to play with loopholes in the so-called "laws of the sea," that, by extension, make treaties irrelevant and arbitrary, re-balancing some of the ongoing territorial claims. The elevations and topographic deformations in the ceramics are fictional, loose interpretations.

DATE: 2016 / PROJECT: LCLA Office, Luis Callejas, Charlotte Hansson / CLIENT: 2016 Oslo Architecture Triennial / PHOTOS: Luis Callejas

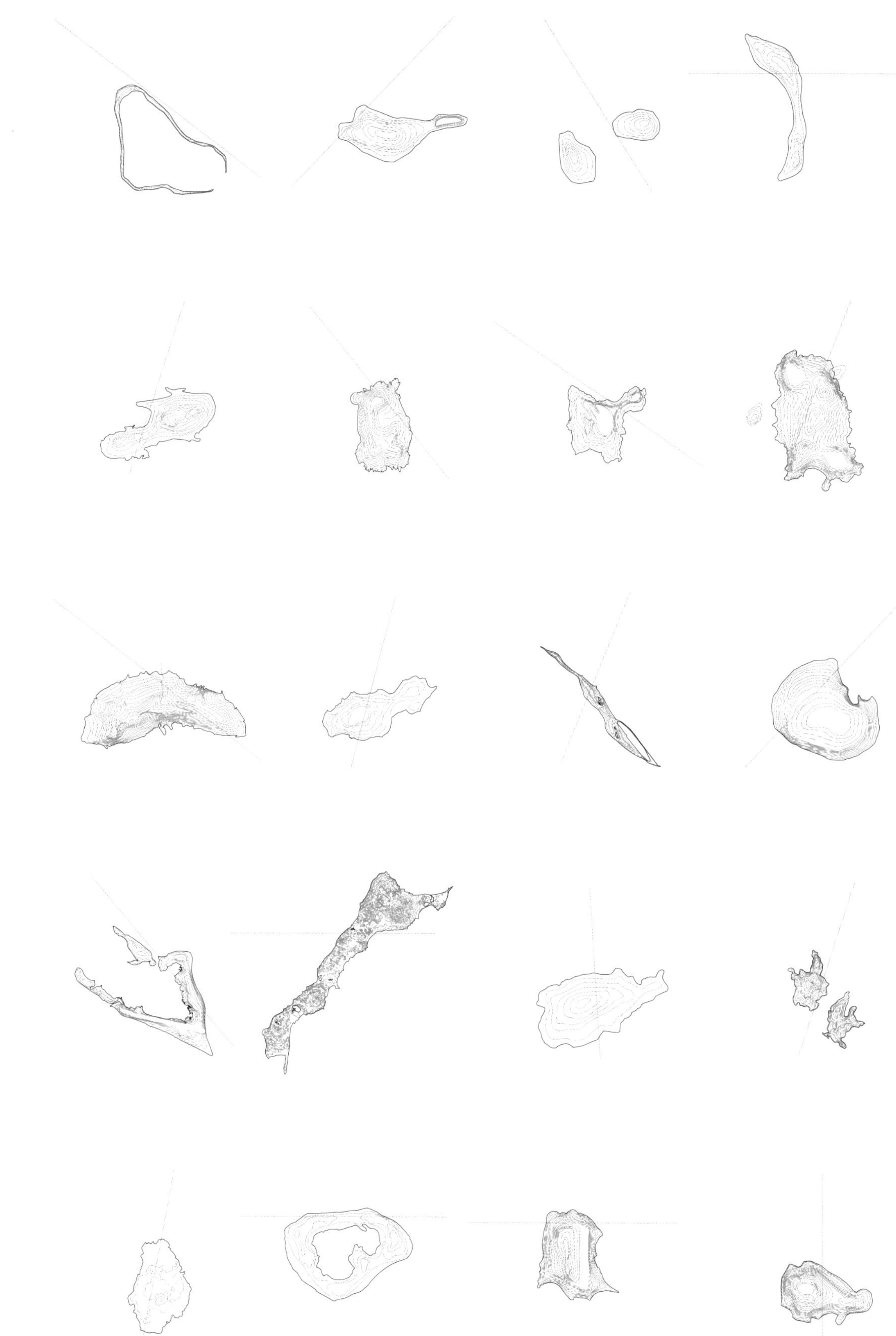

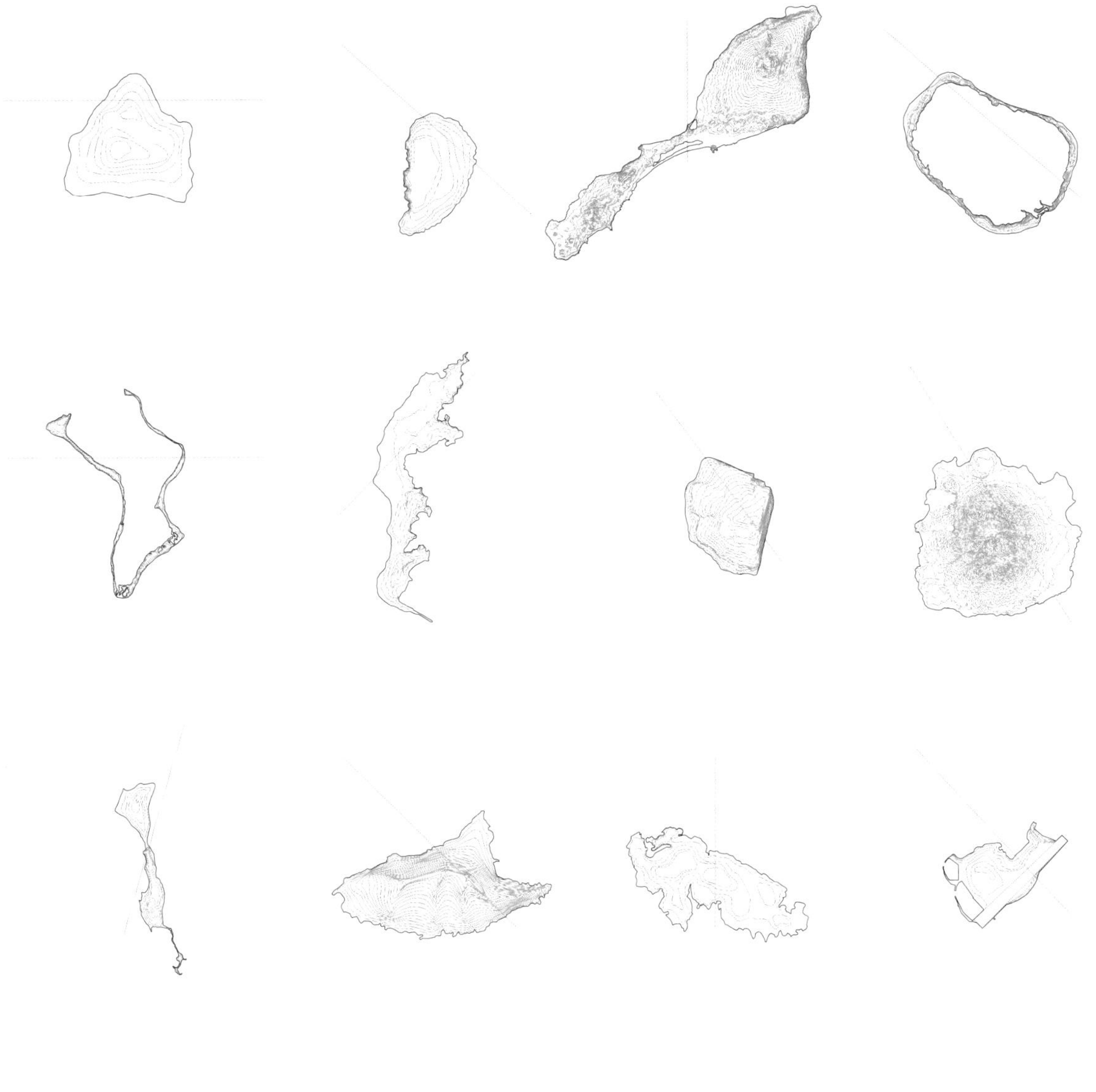

CLIPPERTON
10°18'N 109°13'W
South Pacific Atoll
France vs. Mexico
6 km^2
Top elevation 29 m

MEANGUERA ISLAND
13°10'47'N 87°41'51'W
Gulf of Fonseca
El Salvador vs. Honduras
vs. Nicaragua
23.6 km^2
Top elevation 783 m

SENKAKU ISLANDS / PINNACLE ISLANDS
25°44'41.49'N 123°28'29.79'E
East China Sea
Japan vs. Taiwan
8 islands: 800 m^2 - 4.3 km^2
Top elevation 383 m

SERRANA (ARCHIPELAGO OF SAN ANDRÉS)
12°33'N 81°43'W
Caribbean Sea
Colombia vs. Nicaragua
52.2 km^2
Top elevation 84 m San Andrés,
360 m Providencia, Southwest
Cay 2 m

NAVASSA ISLAND
18°24'10'N 75°0'45'W
Caribbean Sea
Haiti and United States
5.4k m^2 4.7 km x 2.1 km
Top elevation 76 m

MACHIAS SEAL ISLAND
44°30'10'N 67°06'10'W
Gulf of Maine
Canada vs. United States
8 ha
Population two coast guards
running the lighthouse

HANS ISLAND
80°49'41'N 66°27'35'W
Nares Strait between Baffin
Bay and Arctic Ocean
Canada vs. Denmark
1,290 m x 1,199 m

HAWAR ISLANDS
25.60°N 50.77°E
Persian Gulf
Bahrain vs. Qatar
20 islands - 54.5 km^2
Top elevation 22 m
Population 250

WOODY ISLAND (PARACEL ISLANDS)
16°40'N 112°20'E
South China Sea
China vs. Taiwan vs. Vietnam
Archipelago with over 130
features
Top elevation 14 m

WAKE ISLAND
19°18'N 166°38'E
Pacific Ocean
United States vs. Marshall Islands
7.1 km^2
Top elevation 6 m
Population 94

JAN MAYEN
70°59'N 8°32'W
Arctic sea
Norway vs. Greenland (Denmark)
377 km^2
Top elevation: 2,277 m

ROCKALL
57°35'46.695'N 13°41'14.308'W
North-east Atlantic
UK vs. Ireland
784 m^2
Top elevation 17.15 m

MÄRKET
60.301008°N 19.131432°E
Baltic Sea
Sweden vs. Finland
0.35 km x 0.15 km
Population 0

PEREJIL ISLAND
35°54'50'N 5°25'08'W
Strait of Gibraltar
Spain vs. Morocco
15 ha
Top elevation 37 m

IMIA/KARDAK ISLANDS
37°03'03'N 27°09'04'E
Aegean Sea
Greece vs. Turkey
40,000 m^2
Top elevation 6 m

SNAKE ISLAND
45°15'N 30°12'E
Black Sea
Romania vs. Ukraine
0.17 km^2 - 662 x 440 m
Top elevation 41 m

UKATNY ISLAND
45°55'28'N 49°34'40'E
Caspian Sea
Russia vs. Kazakhstan
6.2 x 4.3 km, marsh

SWAINS ISLAND
11°03'20'S 171°04'40'W
Pacific Ocean
United States vs. Tokelau
151 ha low

EL TIGRE ISLAND
13.272°N 87.641°W
Caribbean Sea
Honduras vs. El Salvador vs.
Nicaragua
Top elevation 783 m

ISLA DE TIERRA (ALHUCEMAS ISLANDS)
35.2152°N 3.9026°W
Mediterranean Sea
Considered to be under Spanish
sovereignty, but claimed by Morocco
192 m x 87 m
Top elevation 11 m

LOS MONJES ARCHIPELAGO
12°22'N 70°54'W
Caribbean Sea
Venezuela vs. Colombia
0.2 km^2
Top elevation from South 70 m,
from East 43 m, from North 41 m

DOUMEIRA ISLAND
12.715465°N 43.148044°E
Red Sea
Eritrea vs. Djibouti
1.3 km^2

CORISCO ISLAND
0°55'N 9°19E
Corisco Bay
Gabon vs. Equatorial Guinea
14 km^2
Top elevation 35 m

RUKWANZI ISLAND
1°14'04.9"N 30°28'19.5"E
Lake Albert
Congo vs. Uganda
1,000 m x 600 m

MIGINGO ISLAND
0°52'58'S 33°56'17'E
Lake Victoria
Uganda vs. Kenya
2,000 m^2

GLORIOSO ISLANDS
11°33'S 47°20'E
Indian Ocean
France vs. Seychelles
5 km^2

DIEGO GARCÍA (CHAGOS ARCHIPELAGO)
6°00'S 71°30'E
Indian Ocean
UK vs. Maldives
30 km^2

ST MARTIN'S ISLAND
20°37'38.12'N 92°19'21.28'E
Bay of Bengal
Bangladesh vs. Myanmar
16 km x 0.5 km

BACH LONG VI ISLAND
20°08'N 107°43'E
(Gulf of Tonkin)
Vietnam vs. China
Top elevation 58 m

AVES ISLAND
15°40'18'N 63°36'59'W
Caribbean Sea
Venezuela vs. USA
374 x 50 m
Top elevation 4 m

HUNTER ISLAND
22°22'S 171°43'E
Oceania
France vs. Vanuatu
0.6 km^2
Top elevation 242 m

PEDRA BRANCA
1°19'49'N 104°24'21'E
South China Sea
Singapore vs. Malaysia
137 x 60 m

SCARBOROUGH SHOAL
15°11'N 117°46'E
South China Sea
China vs. Taiwan vs. Vietnam
150 km^2
Top elevation 1.8 m

MATTHEW ISLAND
22°21'S 171°21'E
Oceania
France vs. Vanuatu
0.7 km^2
Top elevation 177 m

KUNASHIR ISLAND (SOUTHERN KURIL ISLANDS)
44°07'N 145°51'E
Sea of Okhotsk
Russia vs. Japan
123 km x 30 km
Top elevation 1,819 m

SOCOTRAN ARCHIPELAGO
12°30'36"N 53°55'12"E
Indian Ocean
Yemen vs. Somalia
132 km x 50 km
Top elevation 1,503 m

MBAÑE
0°48'38.5"N 9°22'43.4"E
Corisco Bay
Gabon vs. Equatorial Guinea
52.5 ha

AL HALLANIYA (KHURIYA MURIYA ISLANDS)
17°30'N 56°00'E
Arabian Sea
Oman vs. Yemen
5 islands

ANCOURT ROCKS
37°14'30'N 131°52'0'E
Sea of Japan
South Korea vs. Japan
16 ha
Top elevation 169 m

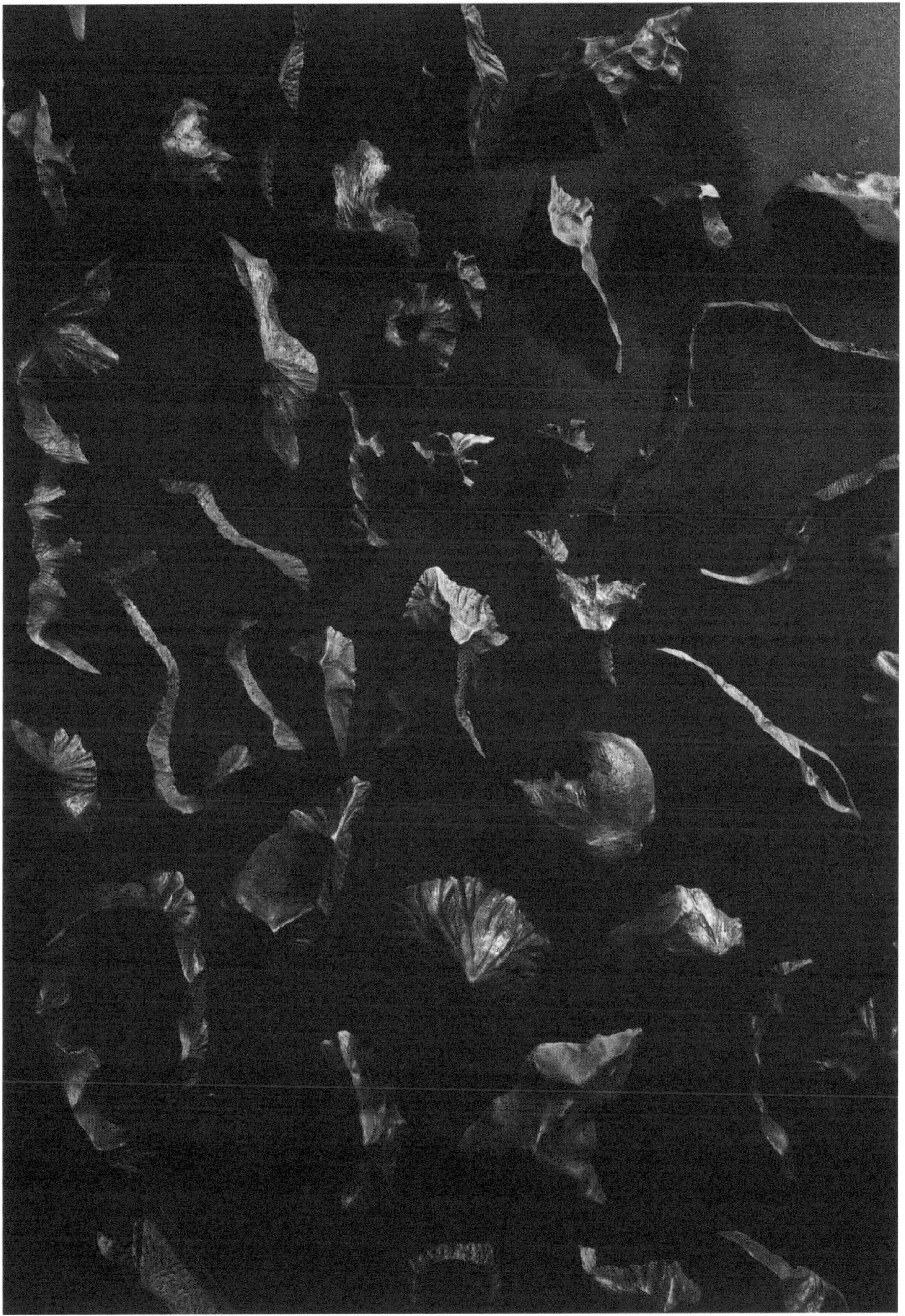

As an infrastructural operation is repeated in different territories, what emerges is a systematic drawing, a pattern of a totality that incorporates both local and universal. Difference is incorporated in a protocol that responds to social, political, economic, and territorial problems through the extension of the aqueducts.

Brazilian Archipelago – All of Brazil Connected by Aqueducts

BRAZIL

Sérgio Bernardes

The aqueducts and waterways proposed by Sérgio Bernardes provide a potential means of development and lay out a possible strategy for Brazil to combat regional disparities in wealth and infrastructure and achieve environmental balance. Based on a detailed study of Brazil's hydrographic system, he proposes a nationwide effort to construct sixteen geometrically organized rings that are connected by 30,000 km of aqueducts. These were planned to be built on existing river beds, in accordance with routes of production, trade, transport, and other uses of water. They would contain power stations and facilities for the treatment of effluents. Aqueducts would unify the nation, integrating its various regions and promoting economic, social, and environmental parity among them. (1)

Pathways of the First Tropical Civilization All of Brazil Connected by Aqueducts

Throughout human history, rivers have always served as natural pathways for the spread of civilization. In a certain way, they were compasses for mankind's progress, pointing out directions, indicating routes for the exploration of the Earth. By way of rivers, man blazed his way into the interior of the continents, built settlements, and made the cities grow. For this reason, and for the wealth that they offer, rivers are one of our most bountiful universal heritages. But in his interventions, man has acted more in a predatory way than with the aim of protecting and preserving rivers' potential. Provoked by these and other ecological attacks, nature has also altered the rivers, changing the course of many of them, generating the dramatic contradictions of droughts and floods, pummeling entire populations, leaving many homeless.

It is now necessary to change the character of man's intervention with rivers. He must tame them while also ensuring that they do not become sources of hunger, misery, or death, but rather of life, abundance, and rebirth. A country's national defense depends in part on the proper care of this universal heritage. It must unite everything in its surroundings with the connection between nature with man, for the benefit of social well-being. In short, the moment to recover the historical role of the river—the pathways of civilization—is now.

In a continental nation such as Brazil, the power of

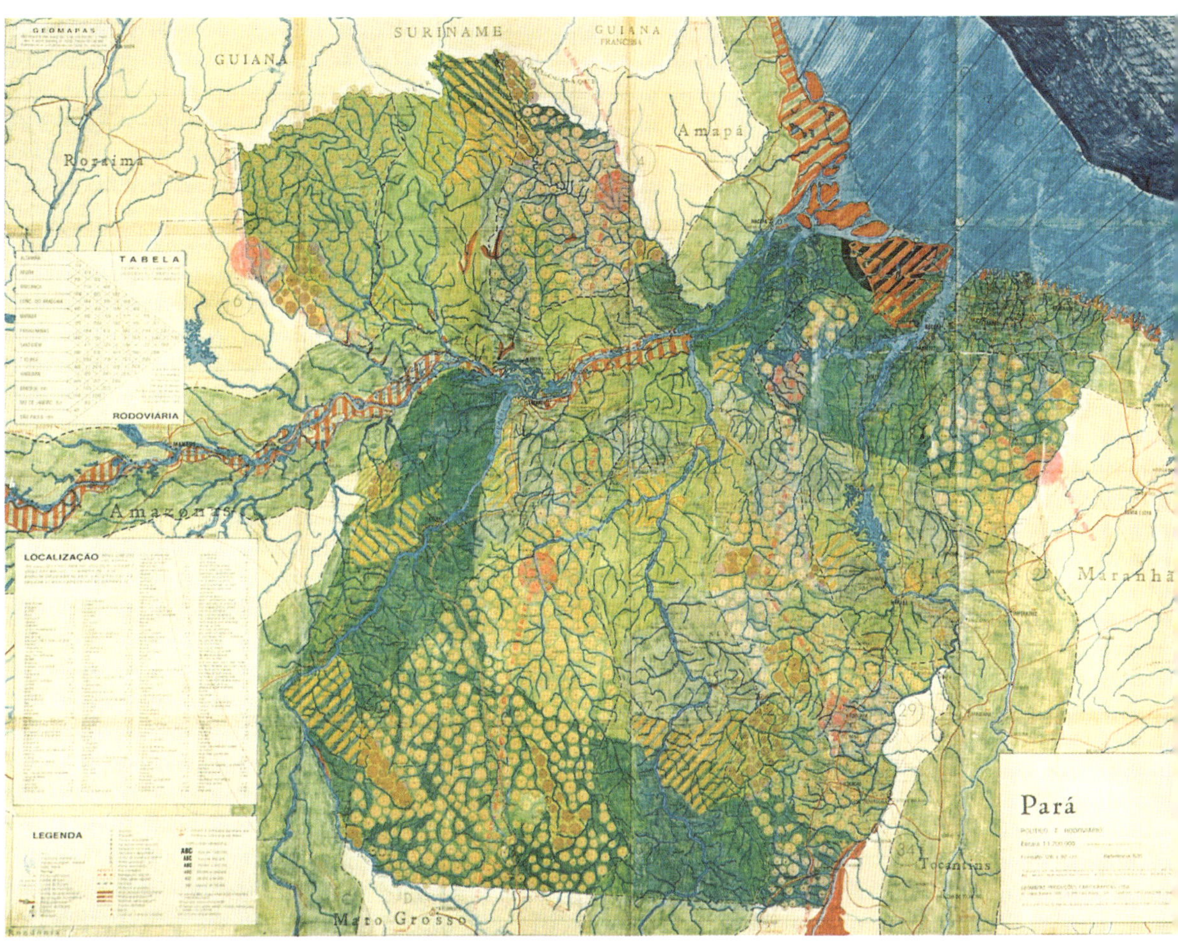

rivers is staggering. We cannot apply models conceived for other contexts to this case; rather we must employ a unique and original alternative designed for Brazilian rivers and with the aim of developing the country as a whole. This means not only developing in privileged areas but throughout the country's territorial vastness; overcoming regional divergences and equitably distributing national wealth; putting an end to the drought in the Northeast and the floods in the South; lowering costs of shipping and travel while also solving the problem of environmental pollution and electrical power generation.

Such wide-ranging and decisive results for the country's future arise from a simple idea, inspired by an age-old practice: aqueducts or *aquavias*. Brazil could interlink all of its rivers through a system of sixteen aqueducts built in the form of a ring, connected in a way that allows their waters to go where they are needed. This would immediately allow for a redistribution of the country's hydric potential.

The largest aqueduct would be more than five hundred kilometers in radius and about three thousand kilometers in perimeter, circling approximately 850 thousand square kilometers in Central Brazil. The smallest one would be the Jequitinhonha Ring, including portions of Bahia and Minas Gerais with a radius of approximately 180 kilometers and an extension of less than 1,200 kilometers. Approximately sixty percent of the Brazilian territory would lie within this set of sixteen rings. In total, there would be thirty thousand kilometers of aqueducts, which would not only transport water, but also serve as routes for shipping merchandise, with space along their edges for implementation of a monorail system for high-velocity passenger trains.

The aqueducts would be built along the river courses, cutting through them or taking advantage of the plains, the valleys, the canyons, the depressions, or the lower slopes of the mountains in order to obviate monumental engineering works without systematic direction. The

LOCATION: Brazil / DATE: 1970 / SITE AREA: 30,000 linear km / PROJECT: Sérgio Bernardes water would be captured by gravity or by suction. It would also flow by gravity or by pressure in a suspended channel measuring twenty meters wide by ten meters deep. Two more channels, one on either side, would run along the edge of this central channel; each measuring twenty-five meters wide by five meters deep. They would simultaneously serve as rain-water collectors and as waterways for the transport of cargo containers.

In these three channels, three types of water would flow: potable, crude water for industrial use, and water for irrigation. Under them, there would be pumping and water-treatment stations. The country needs to wake up to its natural evolution, undertaking a nationwide, collective effort for the construction of new transport routes that are fed by the rivers. With this project, hope would be revived in Brazil.

Building aqueducts by way of a nationwide, collective effort would represent the beginning. Its first effect would be to eliminate unemployment in this nation. And, on these new work fronts, workers would not only receive money but also guarantees of social security; they would have the opportunity to appreciate and closely accompany the construction of a new era for Brazil, obtaining first-hand knowledge of each part of the project.

The aqueducts would be much more than a simple water-supply network. They would bring all the regions closer together, integrating them and linking them, while conjoining natural resources and human efforts with the aim of definitively ending the problems of drought, floods, and pollution. The project would simultaneously create more economical alternatives for transport and power generation. By extension, such a construction effort would not only result in the nation's integration and salvation but would also provide a solution for unemployment and the economic crisis.

(1) Text from Projeto Memoria, Sérgio Bernardes Archive.

(2) Bernardes, Sérgio. "Revolution without the R," in the exhibition at Rio de Janeiro's Modern Art Museum (MAM), 1983, with Bernardes, Kykah and Cavalcanti, Lauro (organizer), Rio de Janeiro: Artviva, 2010, p. 299.

AQUEDUCT SYSTEM: 1960 – 1970

Each fragment of the park is taken in its specificity, its natural form, and the composition speaks to both the individual and the grand. Different programs and uses are planned through a focus on specific zones.

Parque Ecológico Lago de Texcoco

MEXICO

Iñaki Echeverría Gutiérrez

This project identifies landscape as a piece of hydrological infrastructure that is open to the public. Parque Ecológico Lago de Texcoco (Parque Texcoco) aims to direct the future of Greater Mexico City towards a sustainable environmental, political, and social development.

Within the project, landscape is conceptualized as a transformation and evolution of this dynamic territory. Parque Texcoco not only has the potential to constitute an ecological and recreational area but also to serve critical functions that help mitigate the environmental challenges of the city, such as hydrological management, urban flood prevention, temperature regulation, air quality improvement, soil and vegetation rehabilitation and, most importantly, the regeneration of the Lake Texcoco and other water bodies within the Parque Texcoco territory and the larger Valley of Mexico.

This project intends to strategize landscape as an articulation between the urban, the agricultural, and the rural. Parque Texcoco strives to reshape the relationship between territory, city, and water. It seeks to change centuries of conflict between the city and its geography. The 30,300 acres become an opportunity to rethink the territory.

The project engages infrastructure, environmental services, social-infrastructure, and public space at once. It aims to hybridize the traditional notion of infrastructure, generating a more complete and complex understanding of the contemporary ideas of territory and landscape. It will bring the financial and political resources traditionally associated with gray infrastructure to a broader system of green and public landscape, providing not only social and economic resilience but also an enduring management of its spaces.

Other reference projects that have worked naturally with water in cities have also had a significant influence on this plan. These examples allow the natural cycles of floods and droughts to occur in a controlled and designed way, moving away from gray infrastructure to new green infrastructure.

AERIAL VIEW NABOR CARRILLO LAKE PARK

Latin American cities are facing huge challenges related to environmental conflicts, inequality, uncontrolled expansion of urban areas, violence, urban health issues, lack of green spaces, among others. The project will limit urban sprawl in the city through the renovation, protection, and conservation of 12,300 hectares of natural terrain. Environmental and health problems caused by the emission of PM10 particles in the area will also be mitigated, considerably reducing the pollution rates in the Valley of Mexico and its adjacent zones.

Parque Texcoco aims to reduce inequality and violence by improving the living conditions of the inhabitants living near the territory. It will provide public spaces, agricultural and productive areas, and sports and cultural entertainment spaces, which will benefit the most disadvantaged areas of the city that have been historically deprived of green spaces and have suffered high rates of poverty and a lack of social opportunities.

The project represents a broad transformation of the entire Valley of Mexico. It will develop a different sense of history by focusing on creating a better way of living for its inhabitants.

LOCATION: Federal Area of Texcoco Lake, State of Mexico, Mexico / DATE: 2019 / SITE AREA: 12,300 ha / PRINCIPAL ARCHITECT DIRECTOR: Iñaki Echeverría Gutiérrez / ARCHITECTURE: Daniel Holguín Fernández / LANDSCAPE: Pedro Camarena Berruecos INSTITUTION: National Commission of Water (CONAGUA), Parque Ecológico Lago de Texcoco (PELT) / CLIENT: Government of Mexico, Ministry of Environment and Natural Resources / TEXT: Iñaki Echeverría Gutiérrez / IMAGES: Artistic Conceptual Images by PELT

This project represents a unique opportunity to create a hydrological balance while also mitigating health and environmental risks; it will also offer new recreational spaces for residents and visitors. It will provide public spaces, agricultural and productive zones, and sports and cultural entertainment areas. It will improve hydrological management in the region, provide solar energy and its distribution, and contribute to a recovery of landscape in the city.

—Iñaki Echeverría Gutiérrez

This project explores a contemporary take on living from the land as humans and non-humans learn to communicate together by allowing the natural order to come before form.

System of Integrated Patches: Deconstructing the Urban-Rural Limit in the City of Santiago

CHILE

Francisco Walker Martínez

The project System of Integrated Patches: Deconstructing the Urban-Rural Limit in the City of Santiago was commissioned by the metropolitan authority, the borough of San Bernardo, and a local non-profit organization, Santiago Cerros Isla. It aimed to develop a corridor where five hills come together to become a system of natural areas for the city. The main question guiding this commission was: how can a substantial urban project be undertaken with few resources? The answer turned out to be that it could not be done, at least not under the terms of the national competition that commissioned the task. We decided not to interpret the commission as a uniproject but rather as a communicating system. To achieve this, the key was in the landscape: we planned and designed the project by enhancing what was already there instead of forcing ourselves to deliver under the terms defined in the commission. System of Integrated Patches is one of the few projects that did not build a unified corridor or architectural piece. Our decisions were enhanced by the expertise of an anthropologist and a sustainable development specialist, who each brought new visions for addressing landscape. One vision appealed to the idea of a sense of place in relation to landscape, asking, what was it about this part of the territory (and not necessarily the city) that appealed to local identities? The other raised the question of wildlife mobility, of understanding how species move inside the urban system and transition between natural conserved areas and urban spaces; this frame beckoned us to understand the relationships between animal and vegetal species.

The premise of the project does not directly refer to the theme of landscape urbanism as such, though its problematics approach it at a few junctures, and surely shook our professional conventions. The team was composed of young architects trying to unlearn formalism. We realized that form should not be considered first. We grasped that this national architecture competition was not an architectural competition. It could not be so as it is impossible to design five kilometers of public spaces, services, housing zones, and so on as if it were an authorial work. Rather, we had to understand the site's rules, its natural systems of order, and then consider how

to protect them, enhance them or, perhaps, celebrate them. In this way, landscape should shape urbanism before urban design can shape landscape.

As architects and professionals from Latin America, we must allow our professional practice to be nourished by our natural and cultural landscapes. Latin America is not one thing, and it may be a mistake to think there can be a Latin American approach, however, if there is anything we share it is that our cities are young and our built environment has tended to replicate foreign models that are in tension with our natural environment and our native cultures. This is a tension that may be traced back to colonialism, but it is beginning to crack in the context of the climate crisis, opening a great opportunity for our region to offer new ways of thinking about architecture.

LOCATION: San Bernardo, Santiago, Chile / DATE: 2015 / STATUS: Project Research / GROUP LEADER: Francisco Walker Martínez, architect / TEAM: Alejandra Vásquez, Lucas Mateluna, Juan Samaniego, Francisco Salas, architects / COLLABORATORS: Francisco Chatea, Inés Burdiles, architects, Martín Fonck, anthropologist, Santiago Rojas, Sustainable Development Specialist / CLIENTS: Metropolitan Government of Santiago, Municipal Government of San Bernardo, Santiago Cerros Isla NGO / TEXT: Francisco Walker Martínez

1

2

3

1 Cut ype for Cumbres Qualification
2 Hasbún Patch: San Bernardo Campus
3 Adasme Patch: Botanical Garden

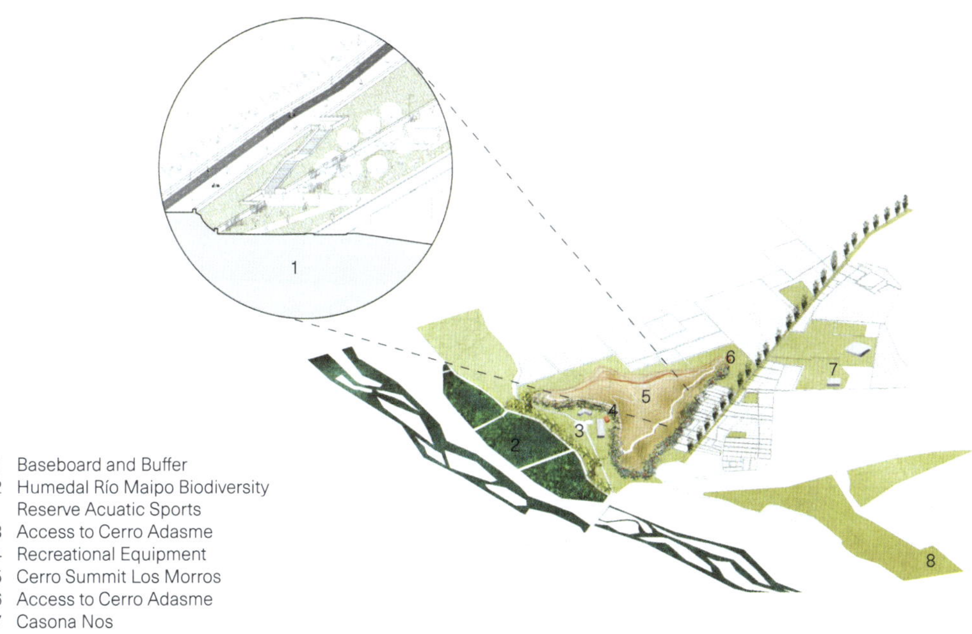

1 Baseboard and Buffer
2 Humedal Río Maipo Biodiversity Reserve Acuatic Sports
3 Access to Cerro Adasme
4 Recreational Equipment
5 Cerro Summit Los Morros
6 Access to Cerro Adasme
7 Casona Nos
8 Maipo Park PRMS 100

The project deconstructs the urban-rural limit as a line and proposes to explore it as it is: landscape. It is a metropolitan transitioning area that aims to protect the identities of rural production activities while at the same time enhancing nature and biodiversity and not compromising urban growth. The buffer zones hosting both recreational and productive activities are extend around each hill. These areas enhance agriculture, recreation, scientific research, and local production activities that can regulate the transition between urban life and natural conservation areas. The project proposes to conserve and enhance the ecological values that each one—of the twenty-six island hills that emerge within the urban landscape in Santiago—represents by preserving their bodies through native species reforestation and a few interpretative paths for hiking. Protecting these natural areas against urban predation, along with enhancing them as places for recreation and natural conservation, has been at the center of multiple agendas in the last decade.

Flirting between the specific and the general, Common Places builds a framework from a cultural perspective. What its many iterations represents is not necessarily a democratic system, but instead a medium for negotiating relationships in a globalized world.

Common Places

CHILE

Plan Común

Common Places is an international and collaborative research project initiated and promoted by the architecture office Plan Común. It is based in Santiago, Chile. For the last forty years, neoliberal experiments have been ongoing in Chile. The project focuses on the discussion and production of formal strategies to maximize collective space. It is an attempt to establish a common structure for dialogue and exchange, avoiding competition and fragmentation among a group of architects in order to openly discuss, through our discipline and knowledge, issues related to our built environment, culture, and commons. The group focuses on specific subjects that give shape to our everyday life and environments: from micro interventions to urban transformations; from landscape to infrastructure; from representation to monumentality.

Common Places is a hybrid between a compilation and a curatorial process: it is an exercise to introduce and delineate new narratives, protocols, and habits. The aim was not to express a creative freedom without limits nor explore a bold pragmatism but instead to convey a "corrective architecture," as defined by Elias Zenghelis, "that would make sense to its occupants." (1) It brings about a compilation of strategies that could be used as a manual, to be appropriated, manipulated, and translated in different political and cultural contexts in order to reinforce the collective realm. In the end, we all agreed on the fact that "for an architect, architecture is active propaganda in the original sense of the word." (2)

Collaboration and cooperation are an integral part of practicing architecture, and this research was also an attempt to prove it. Of course, we would have much more to say and design if we were able to build "poor architecture" (3) through a collective force instead of perpetuating an elitist position and maintaining a deliberate level of irreverence and, consequently, irrelevance.

This research came to a close just as a new wave of global authoritarianism, with strong reverberations in Latin America, began its rise. The collective realm is one of this authoritarianism's first victims; it is deactivated to make way for the violent expansion of neoliberalism. Common

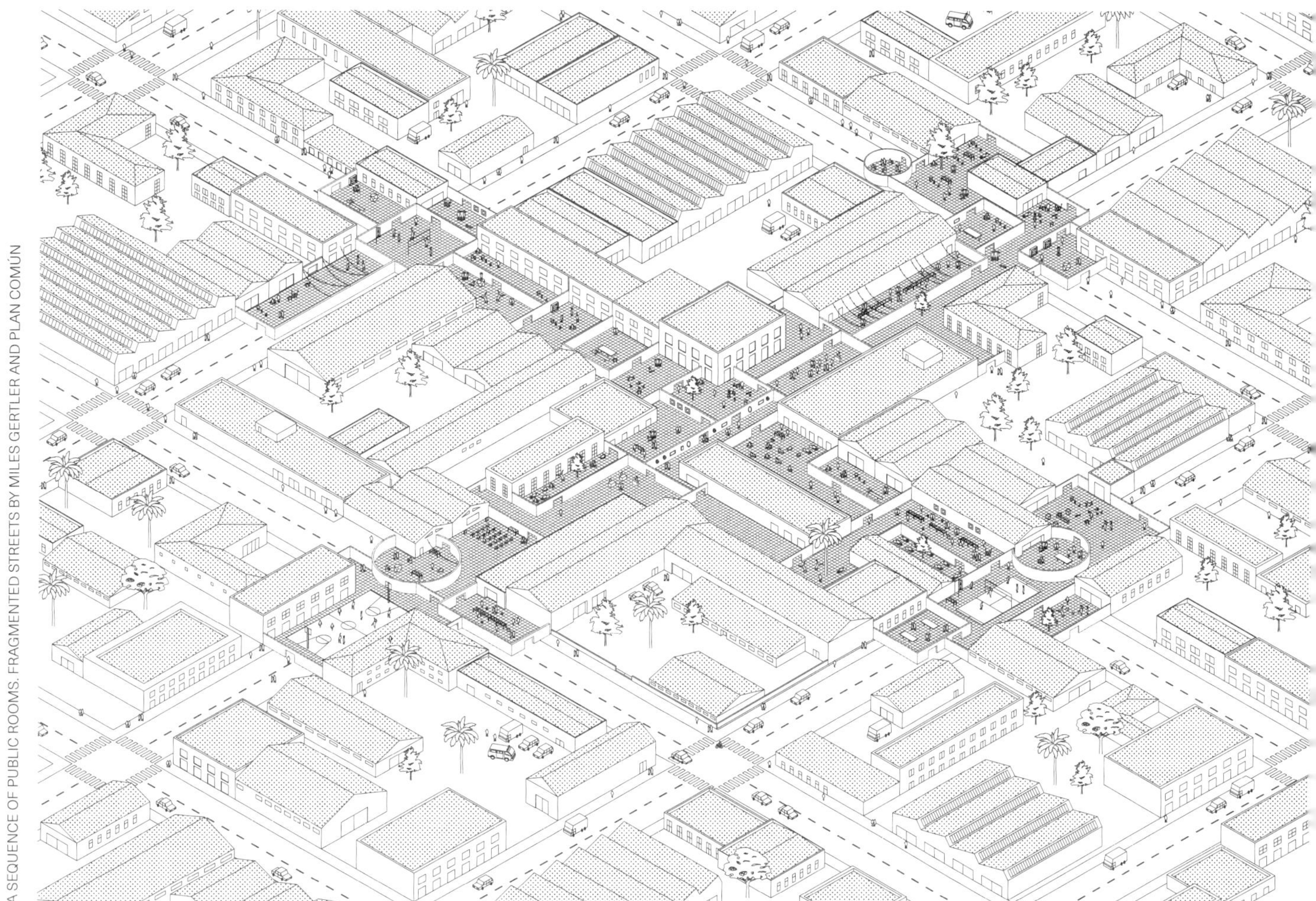

A SEQUENCE OF PUBLIC ROOMS. FRAGMENTED STREETS BY MILES GERTLER AND PLAN COMÚN

sense is precisely what is at stake in the present socio-ecological crisis: a critical architectural project is not just desirable, it is necessary. Through a critical attitude towards physical and cultural contexts—as well as briefs and clients—architecture can appropriate reality in radical and unexpected ways, making visible its potential and its contradictions and developing projects that enable emancipatory ideas to occupy space. As Anselm Jappe has stated, "The task of all the forces that are recognized in the social emancipation project is to find alternatives, prepare for post-capitalism. It matters little that it is called communism, anarchy, emancipated society, or other names." Latin America and the rest of the world must face a concrete scenario, first as citizens and then as architects, and, what is best, as architectural citizens.

(1) Zenghelis, Elias. The Aesthetics of the Present, in AD profile 72, Vol. 58 3/4, 1988.

(2) Zenghelis, Elias, ibid.

(3) "poor architecture not in the sense of poverty, but in the sense of handicraft expressing maximum communication and dignity through minor and humble means." Bo Bardi, Lina. The Pompeia Factory(1986), in Cidadela da Liberdade: Lina Bo Bardi e o SESC Pompeia, Organização de Andre Vainer e Marcelo Ferraz, São Paulo: Edições SESC SP, 2013. Translated by the authors.

LOCATION: Worldwide / DATE: 2012 - 2018 / AUTHORS: Felipe De Ferrari (CL), Kim Courreges (FR), Thomas Batzenschlager (FR), Diego Grass (CL), Marcelo Cox (CL), Jose Lemaitre (CL), Oliver Burch (CH), Costanza Zeni (IT), Jules Salmon (FR), Kotaro Shimada (JP), Pedro Correa (CL), Cristian Valenzuela (CL), Pedro Hoffmann (CL), Luca Magagni (IT), Osvaldo Larraín (CL), Eduardo Corales (CL), Ciro Miguel (BR), Bruna Canepa (BR), Hamed Khosravi (Behemoth, IR), Arturo Scheidegger and Ignacio García Partarrieu (Umwelt, CL), Cruz García and Nathalie Frankowski (Wai Think Tank, CR / FR), Miles Gertler (CA), Erica Chladová and Robert van der Pol (Liminal Office, NL), Javiera Jadue and Paula Livingstone (CL), Tomás Tironi and Christian Bartlau (CL), Cristóbal Amunátegui and Alejandro Valdés (CL), Benjamin Gallegos Gabilondo (CL), Grupo Toma (CL), Fosbury Architecture (IT), Sebastián Paredes (CL), Felipe Grallert (CL), Alejandra Celedón (CL) and Jack Self (EN) / TEXT: Plan Común

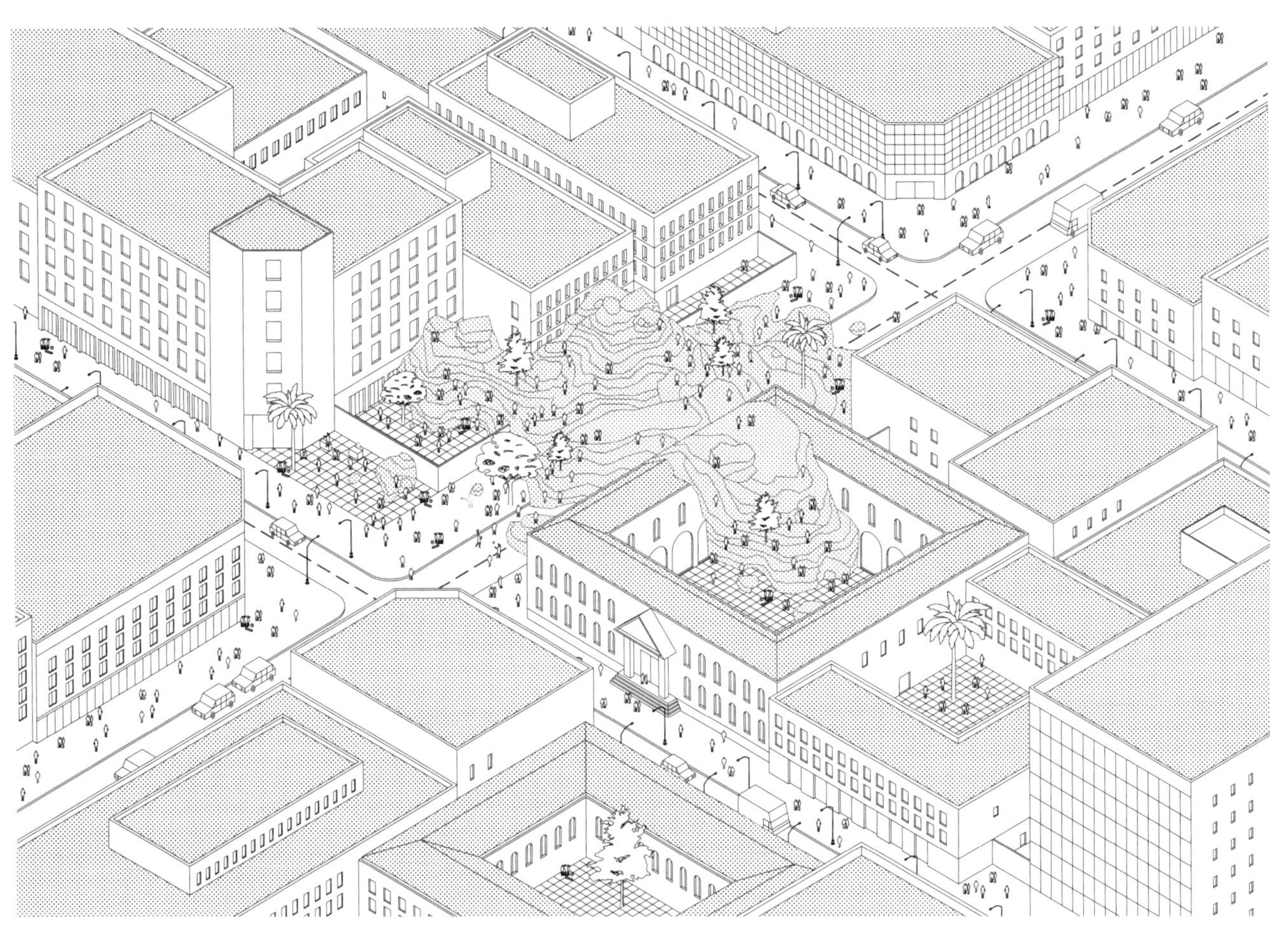

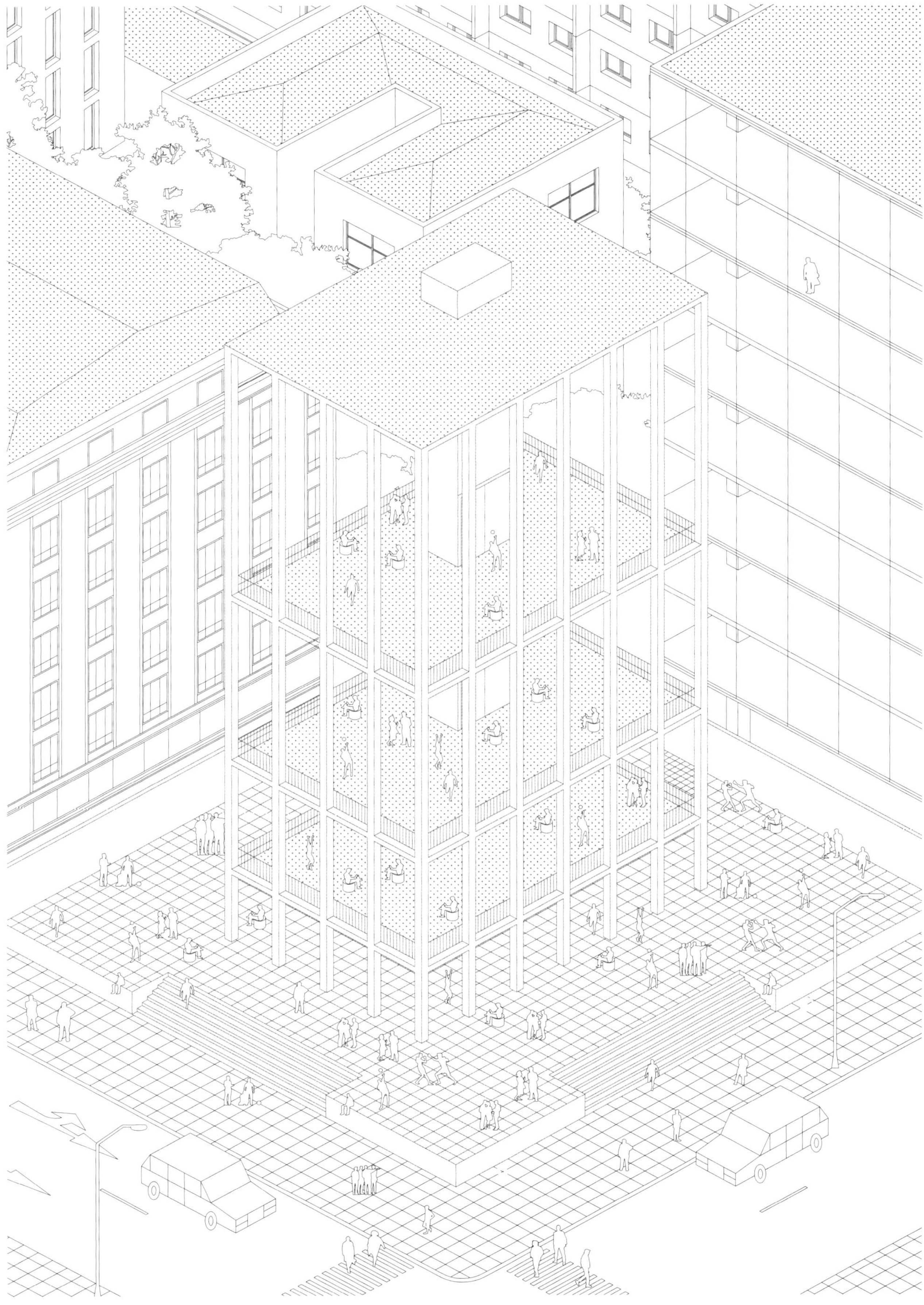

OPEN COLLECTIVE SPACES IN THE AIR. PUBLIC BUILDING BY PLAN COMÚN

Assembled Natures

These projects use nature as a way to rethink the integration of architectural intervention with existing resources. Here, landscape urbanists seek less-explicit ways of drawing boundaries and less-invasive or permanent forms of intervention. These contexts and design procedures are characterized by two different strategies. One uses natural representation patterns to build footprints, incorporating botany-inspired concepts in the development of geometric configurations along with new ideas about urban development, identity, and place-making. The other disrupts the understanding of nature as scenery or picturesque backdrop, blurring the gap between hinterland and urban.

—Mercedes Peralta

Abstract by Nature

LUIS CALLEJAS

The links between late modernist architects and the origins of environmental or ecological design sensitivities are well traced and have recently gained renewed relevance. One story of particular importance is the link between some of the late Bauhaus architects exiled in London and their different intense intellectual exchanges with biologists and naturalists. The Norwegian historian of environmental sciences Peder Anker traced this under-explored history in his short and fascinating book "From Bauhaus to Eco House." Anker argues that, typically, Bauhaus would not be considered an environmentally sensitive moment for design; in fact, one of the widely accepted critiques of Bauhaus is its lack of relevance for contemporary ecological concerns. Anker suggests, however, that it was precisely in the late Bauhaus period in London where some of the most influential early ideas of environmental design emerged. He builds the story of how this sensitivity emerged from the vital and intense relationships between these architects and the scientists they befriended. It is a story of love, parties, affairs, friendships, and genuine collaborations between designers and scientists. Eloquent and refined examples from this period include projects like Berthold Lubetkin's beautiful penguin pool and events like the London discussions on how to better design zoos or botanical gardens.

I want to suggest that a similar story could be told about a particular sensitivity in Latin America at the end of the 20th century. It is recent, yet clearly linked to the late modernist project in tropical contexts. Modernist design canons clashed violently with tropical landscapes, sometimes with negative environmental implications; however, somehow, even some of the most urbanized lush landscapes resisted the heavy handedness frequently attributed to late modernists. In fact, after many decades, the strong material presence of some of these buildings, like those of Lina Bo Bardi, Paulo Mendes da Rocha, or Rogelio Salmona, is seen as a necessary form of establishing an equivalent relationship with such robust environments. This is a landscape where the cycle of life is not interrupted by the winter, where if left alone, vegetation would happily take over more discrete architecture.

It would be a terrible mistake to claim that tropical landscapes do not need protection and care; rather, the point here is that a particularly heavy-handed architecture, mistakenly described as insensitive, has been necessary to promote stewardship of the landscape. The best examples of tropical modernism also catalyzed incredibly talented landscape architects as they had to stand in between strong buildings and even stronger natural environments. It was no coincidence that this context gave origin to original and irreplaceable figures like Roberto Burle Marx.

In a context that often lacks a robust and autonomous landscape education, at least when compared to North America and Europe, knowledge gaps have been filled by methodical and intense collaborations between architects and scientists/naturalists. These collaborations have effectively supplanted the influence of the most dominant landscape traditions. Among the group of architects brought together as contributors to this issue of –NESS. docs, for example, none come from a background of formal landscape training, with the exception of Teresa Moller. Yet, they are all committed, in these projects at least, to engage with landscape as media, if not as landscape architects, then clearly as landscape curators. In many ways, they are not that different from Lubetkind with his beautiful penguin pool, or Cedric Price with his aviary.

Luis Callejas *is the founder of LCLA office and Full Professor of Landscape Architecture at the Oslo School of Architecture and Design. The studio is based in Oslo and is led by Colombian architect and landscape architect Luis Callejas and Swedish architect Charlotte Hansson. Luis Callejas taught architecture and landscape architecture at Harvard GSD (2011-2016). In 2018, Callejas was the Patrick Geddes fellow at the University of Edinburgh. Recently LCLA's work was exhibited at the Chicago Architecture Biennial, the Lisbon Architecture Triennial, Seoul Biennial, and the 2018 Venice Biennial. LCLA's works include the Aquatic Center for the 2010 South American Games, and more recently, the landscape for the renovation of the former US Embassy in Oslo, designed by Eero Saarinen.*

One of the clearest examples of contemporary collaboration between architecture and the natural sciences is Felipe Mesa from Medellín (Plan:B Arquitectos); in fact, Mesa was the first architect in Colombia that declared his practical and intellectual commitment to the ecological project. Years before his project for the Orquideorama, Felipe was experimenting with geometry, writing and constructing in relation to tree forms. His particular interest in modules and repetition seemed to have an ambiguous origin; he was clearly influenced by his studies in Spain, his fascination for Enric Miralles, and later, the writings of Serres and other French thinkers central to environmental discourse. His influences were also coming from his friends, architects from Madrid that, like him, invoked ecology; they were in turn influenced by Ábalos y Herreros and Juan Navarro Baldeweg.

What is remarkable about Felipe Mesa's work is his early interest in real projects, meaning that his studies of nature, systems, modularity, and repetition were not open-ended, academic, or purely speculative, they are more similar to Utzon's additive architecture than they are to Madrid's activist architecture. We know that some of Felipe Mesa's contemporaries from Madrid were, in fact, very critical of building at the same time that he was landing large projects in Colombia, projects of a scale atypical for his young age. He was pushed to operationalize his fascination while his intellectual ambitions generated a kind of friction with reality. A story with similarities to that of the London Bauhaus group is that of Felipe's collaboration with biologist María José Sanin. Sanin was extremely influential in the formation and sharpening of the architect's concepts linked to the natural sciences. I like to think that Sanin's influence is actually more significant than that of his Spanish contemporaries or fellow Colombian architects. Felipe was the first architect in Colombia to horizontally credit a scientist partner as part of many projects. The Orquideorama is clearly part of the crystallization of this process.

Felipe's sketches of the Orquideorama are particularly beautiful; they exist between speculation and construction. They have imprecise lines between figuration and abstraction—like hybrids of plants and animals—while at the same time containing glimpses of clever construction methods. Years after finishing Orquideorama, Felipe and María José Sanin are continuing this collaboration, researching the links between plants and architecture.

Jardín Botánico Medellín, by Vélez Villa and Castro Jaramillo is another fascinating example. As a project it is a threshold, a zone that both separates and connects (depending on the time of the day) the precious collection of the botanical garden with the dense and mineral city fabric of Medellín. The task of designing such a threshold was difficult. Vélez Villa is clearly one of the most refined architects in recent decades in Colombia, while Castro Jaramillo is perhaps the living architect that has been working with landscape as a media for the longest time in the country. The project had to be able to enclose the garden, to control access, while at the same time acting as public space, as a face of the garden towards the city.

Direct references to leaves and botanical motifs adorn the pavement, becoming the only moments where the architects allow for literal representation; other than that, the project is a band that expands and contracts to create spaces that are interesting for the city outside of the garden. The intelligence of the project is that the architects did not fall in the easy temptation to focus all design efforts inwards, creating beautiful spaces for the garden, which is obviously already beautiful as it is spatially defined by the dense botanical collection. The architects generously decided to engage the hard, polluted and noisy urban side, which speaks to their commitment to public space and expresses a generosity that transforms the botanical garden into a space with urban qualities extending outside its own boundaries. The architects here had the support of the botanical garden's full-time scientific staff, who were involved in the renovation and were asked to work closely with the selected architects, including myself; I was, at the time, working in my first job as an architect, sharing an office for two years with the herbarium staff and the house botanists.

Your Reflection, the pavilion by Guillermo Hevia García and Nicolás Urzúa in Chile is an interesting example of a project that wants to work with nature in a design culture and context where other architects are already masters of inspiration and nature adaptation. Here it is important to recall that there is a clear difference between getting inspiration from nature, or finding clever ways to adapt to strong landscapes, and the daunting task of actually using nature as a dominant material.

Your Reflection was temporary and had the rare and privileged opportunity of using plants and light as both form and content. Hevia García and Urzúa, one of the most promising young offices in Chile, had the humble yet strong idea of letting the constructed garden be the main protagonist of their intervention. They designed a garden protected by invisible reflective walls. It is a project for two audiences: the public, who can easily miss the geometry by enjoying the gardens, and architects, who will perhaps enjoy the geometry in the reading of the drawings. Fellow architects are probably going to be audiences ever appreciating the elegant garden's plan only as it appears in publications.

The Memorial a las Víctimas de Violencia en Mexico by Gaeta Springall Arquitectos is located in the second largest urban park in Latin America, clearly Mexico City's most prominent park. By defining a field of walls, the architects not only resisted the cliché of creating a pavilion in the park but also focused on enhancing the experience of the historical park as it is. The field of walls defines the memorial, and what is in fact more interesting, is the open spaces between the walls, which are unusually generous for a memorial. These spaces are what the architects describe as "absence," but in a deft move, they are filled with curated dense views of the monumental trees that surround the memorial. The project ultimately succeeds in incorporating the very old trees into a new project, achieving what many landscape architects would envy: having mature trees from the first day the memorial is open.

Finally, Punta Pite, clearly the most elegant landscape project to appear in Latin America in the past few decades, has very little to do with urbanism; in fact, as I learned when I visited for the first time, it is part of a private coastal development. Moller, decided in this case to work with mineral material. The primitive traces on the rocky coast required a delicate and exquisite survey. This project is an excellent example of how landscape, when carefully designed, can create a world of its own without seeming overly designed. Its length, and even its location, does not matter that much, the ocean here is any ocean, or even better, the project presents an archetype of the coast as landscape. It is an antidote to the brutal urbanization of the coast, (perhaps that was its hidden urban ambition). Once inside, it is easy to forget that this is a privatized coast with no public access to the water's edge.

The most astonishing aspect of the project is its impeccable craft, which is rare for such an intricate and primitive approach to form. One fascinating contradiction is that even if the author often claims that all of her work emerges from the site, this path has such quirky moments that the designer's hand is sometimes stronger than the dramatic existent conditions. In Punta Pite, the only landscape architect of this chapter, ironically, is also the one that brings the most architectural archetypes. In the stairs, which have almost domestic dimensions, the geologic and the typological somehow find a harmonic middle ground of curated views.

Through the architects listed here, and many more young studios in Latin America, we can find varied stories of collaboration with naturalists. It is no exaggeration to say that Latin America offers a story not unlike that of the London Bauhaus naturalist.

A module that could be repeated infinitely functions as the basis of an ecosystem that promotes flexibility, openness, and permeability. This building/pavilion/piece-of-landscape sets the scenario for new partial agreements.

Orquideorama

COLOMBIA

Plan:B Arquitectos, JPRCR Arquitectos

For Plan:B Arquitectos, buildings, the city, and the landscape are the temporary consolidation of natural, social, and urban forces that occur at various scales and with different impacts. Everything is connected through energy and material networks and there are no relevant differences between the natural and the artificial world. The Orquideorama in Medellín's Botanical Garden follows the logic of the surrounding native forest and simultaneously consolidates a flexible and permeable public space. Columns like hollow trunks concentrate structural forces, water networks, energy, and gardens. The roof acts as a translucent and modular foliage that adapts to the position and height of the existing trees. As a whole, it defines a permeable and ambiguous space, available for varied day and night events including concerts, weddings, gastronomic festivals, fairs, and orchid exhibitions. This building is part of a network of public and natural spaces in the city.

We understand the architecture project as a partial agreement (1), and we work with the concept of permeability (2) at different scales of tropical ecosystems. We are interested in flexibility, the availability of public space, and the commitment to ecological practices. On the one hand, we have been influenced by the intelligence behind the architecture of the low-income neighborhoods in Medellín's slopes, their growth strategies, their material diversity, and their intense use of common spaces. On the other, we found inspiration in the bioclimatic and temporary strategies used in lightweight architecture for greenhouses to cultivate flowers, fruits, and vegetables in the Andes Mountains in Colombia.

From our point of view, the biggest challenges of Latin American societies are a need for greater equity, quality education, and ecological empathy. These could also be some of our disciplinary challenges. Our practice in Colombia has been carried out on three fronts with different implications. When we make public and private buildings in cities, the challenges are to consolidate the urban grid, offer communities public space, and connect the buildings with the local landscape. When we make public schools in rural areas, the most important thing is to create durable buildings that respect the natural environment and that allow for changing programs and users. When we design private houses in suburban areas, we give strength to the bioclimatic performance, to the choice of sustainable materials and a careful relationship with the natural environment (3). Also, in our academic activities, we participate in studios that focus on the design of public buildings for low-income communities as well as design-build studios focusing on rural areas of Colombia, where, with our students, we build small wooden buildings useful for diverse communities (4).

(1) Mesa, Felipe and Bernal, Alejandro. "Acuerdos Parciales. Plan:B Arquitectos," Medellín: Mesa Editores, 2005.

(2) Mesa, Felipe and Mesa, Federico. "Permeability. Plan:B Arquitectos," Medellín: Mesaestandar Editores, 2013.

(3) Mesa, Felipe and Mesa, Federico. "Architecture in Reverse. Plan:B Arquitectos," Medellín: Mesaestandar Editores, 2017.

(4) Mesa, Felipe and Mesa, Miguel. "Nubes de Madera," Medellín: Mesaestandar Editores, 2017

LOCATION: Medellín, Colombia / DATE: 2006 / SITE AREA: 4,200 sqm, 45,208.42 sf / DESIGN TEAM: Plan:B Arquitectos, Felipe Mesa, Alejandro Bernal; JPRCR Arquitectos, Camilo Restrepo, J. Paul Restrepo, Viviana Peña, Catalina Patiño, Carolina Gutiérrez, Lina Gil, Jorge Buitrago PROJECT MANAGEMENT: Plan:B Arquitectos; JPRCR Arquitectos / CONSULTANTS: Germán Serrate, structural engineer; Ménsula S.A., construction supervision / CLIENT: Botanical Garden of Medellín / TEXT: Plan:B Arquitectos / PHOTOS: Iwan Baan (pp. 159 and 164), Cristóbal Palma (p. 163)

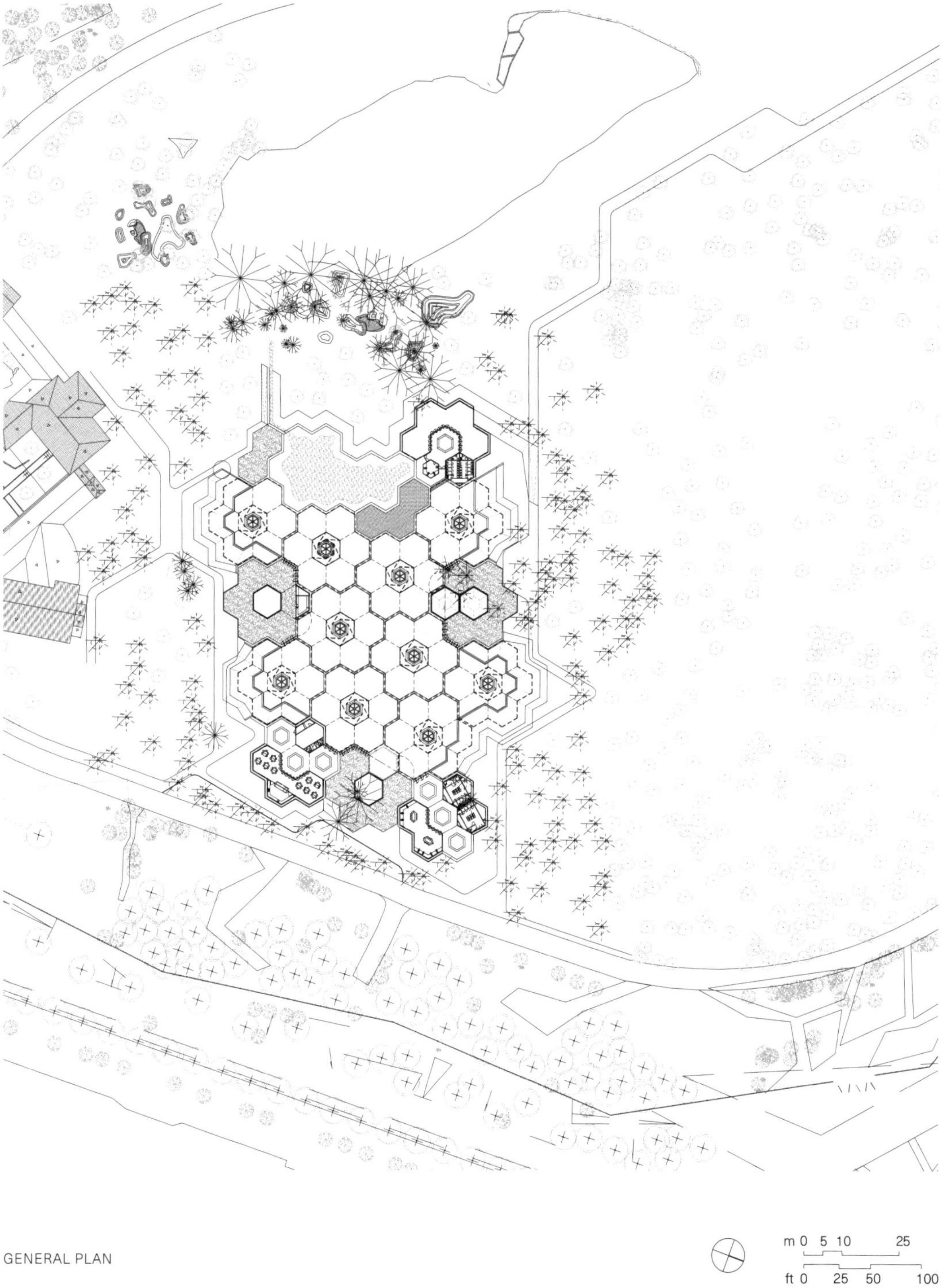

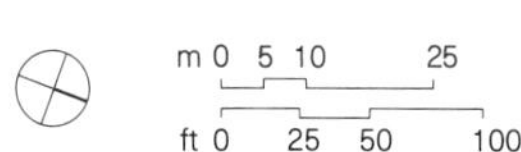

GENERAL PLAN

FLOWER MODULE

ADAPTION AND GROWING

ADAPTION AND GROWING

CONCAVITIES

SPECIES

SERVICES

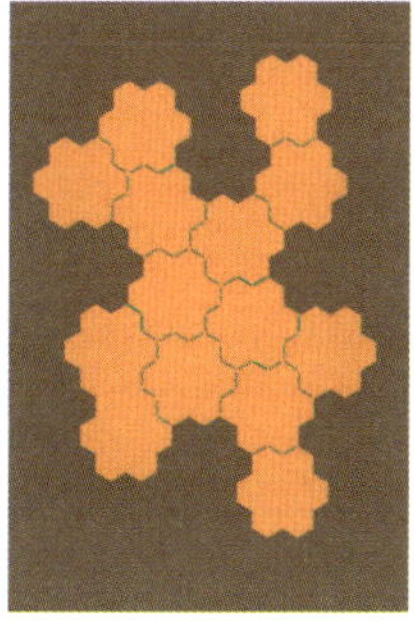
PARTITIONS

NATURAL LIGHT

ARTIFICIAL LIGHT

EXISTING INTERIOR TREES

FLOOR PATTERN

ONGOING EVENTS EXAMPLE

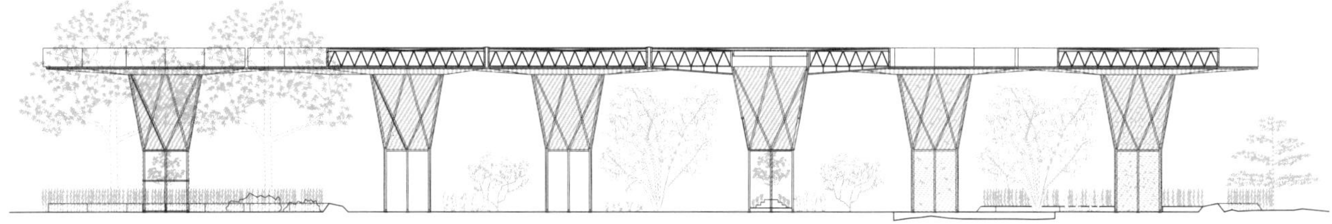

SECTION

The intelligence of the pattern is amplified through repetition but the spatial and bioclimatic qualities are already present in each individual pattern. You could say that the qualities of the pattern emerge from the inside out.

—Plan:B Arquitectos

Active perimeter limits oscillate between the permeable and the formed, rethinking what a boundary can be. A center point, a circular shaped café, is made to reinforce the importance of program.

Jardín Botánico Medellín, Perímetro y Café del Bosque

COLOMBIA

Ana Elvira Vélez Villa, Lorenzo Castro Jaramillo

The notion of landscape has been associated with greenery and gardening in Colombia, and in most of Latin America; however, our joint practice understands landscape as a conscious setting up of a place through a landscape that is inhabited by the human being, enabling urban life to unfold within it; a place where there is an integral coexistence between the urban and the natural context. This is the case of the Jardín Botánico Medellín, where landscape constitutes the project itself, allowing for an articulation of a site that for years was totally isolated from its urban environment. Landscape guides the reorganization of the urban border, which starts from the entrance pavilion (Café del Bosque) and extends around the fourteen hectares of the botanical garden.

The intervention has mainly consisted of the elimination of old enclosures that sheltered the natural space, opening the garden to the city and turning its perimeter into a linear park where the pedestrian can interact with nature and the urban condition of the new border. This intervention aims to generate a strong link between nature and the urban city. The entrance pavilion reaffirms this condition of landscape; it is a threshold that prepares the pedestrian, as he passes through an empty mineral courtyard, to enter the garden, leaving behind the urban conglomeration; an elliptical plan defined by two reinforced concrete walls move and overlap each other, generating an interior space that contains a sheet of water. With a reflection of the sky and the walls, this sheet de-materializes the building boundaries and creates a unique atmosphere.

We face each project as the opportunity to create new places for life, inserting new pieces in existing environments and cities and thus building new relationships, new architectures, new landscapes. A number of international artists have inspired us, including Richard Long, Richard Serra, Christo and Jeanne-Claude, and Andy Goldsworthy. These artists transform places into new landscapes that never existed before. In Colombia, we are motivated by artists like Eduardo Ramírez Villamizar, with geometric pieces that stand alone in the landscape, Carlos Rojas, who appropriates geographical environments with simple pieces, Hugo

Zapata, who builds cosmogonic places, or Luis Fernando Peláez, whose landscapes draw upon memory and travel. Last but not least, pre-Columbian architecture serves as an inspiration for the construction of new landscapes, of configuring systems of architectural pieces and empty spaces. In the case of the Jardín Botánico Medellín, a new urban border was proposed. The topography was accompanied throughout its length by self-supporting and transparent enclosure modules that run through the space like a large snake and coalesce with the entrance pavilion, the Café del Bosque; these form a system that builds the urban edge, which is fundamentally kinetic, by activating the movement of people who travel in the subway and walk from the *comunas*. It proposes a live urban edge that allows the Jardín Botánico Medellín to be articulated in the city and values its condition as an urban piece that builds a new landscape.

Perhaps the challenge for Latin American cities is to recognize that the existing systems and structures are disjointed, exclusive and inequitable; there is a need to find pieces that can complete our cities and turn them into inclusive landscapes. The Jardín Botánico Medellín exists since 1969, but it was absent from the urban structure due to the tall white walls that completely enclosed and isolated it. Our work was to insert this urban piece into the city, not only replacing the wall with a transparent enclosure module, but also by creating a new landscape that articulated the existing city with the interior garden.

By allowing the city to caress the garden and the garden to caress the city, a non-existent landscape was built that contained the strength of an encounter between city, mountains, and garden.

LOCATION: Medellín, Colombia / STARTING DATE: 2005 / FINAL DATE: 2007 / SITE AREA: 28,515 sqm, 307,320.41 sf / STATUS: Built
DESIGN TEAM: Ana Elvira Vélez Villa, Lorenzo Castro Jaramillo, architects / COORDINATOR: Jhenny Nieto, architect / COLLABORATORS: Eliana Beltrán, Julia Cano, Juan Camilo Vaquero, Andrés Castro, architects / CONSULTANTS: German Zerrate, Jaime Andrés Ortega, engineers / CLIENT: Jardín Botánico Medellín Joaquín Antonio Uribe, Secretary of Public Developments of Medellin Government
PHOTOS: Isaac Ramírez (p. 167), Sergio Gómez (p. 168)

JARDIN

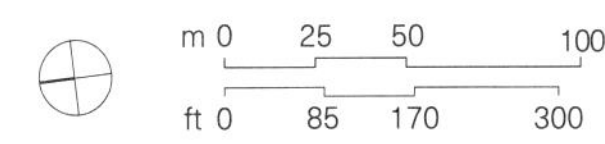

GENERAL PLAN

The void in the middle of the urban appears as an opportunity to concentrate past memories. It raises a voice that is materialized in the metal plates and commemorates victims with each passing through it.

Memorial a las Víctimas de la Violencia en México

MEXICO

Gaeta Springall Arquitectos

When we saw the site, we knew it had to be a forest; in more than one way, the existing landscape suggested how the space had to be arranged. Landscape plays a fundamental role in the city and the Memorial a las Víctimas de Violencia en México is an urban piece that respects the site's pre-existing characteristics.

The landscape as urbanism framework plays an important role in the Gaeta Springall Arquitectos' agenda. Examples include the Memorial a las Víctimas de Violencia as well as the Parque Lineal Ferrocarril de Curnavaca. The office is currently involved in several projects related to the improvement of public spaces in the Iztapalapa Municipality in Mexico City. As an office, we believe that being involved in matters of landscape as urbanism not only improves our capacities of understanding space but also enables us to impact a wider array of people. Las Torres de Satélite by Luis Barragán and Mathias Goeritz deeply influences our work, particularly its dichotomy of massiveness and lightness; that work also inspired this memorial. The most critical present and future challenges for Latin American cities are related to its populations' socioeconomic inequalities. When designing public spaces, this becomes an important aspect to take into consideration as people need to relate to and interact in a context that feels safe. Prior to designing the Memorial a las Víctimas de Violencia, we first had to investigate the subject of violence in Mexico, which made us reflect on victims from a variety of crimes. These thoughts and the ideas were then translated into a drawing that involved shapes and voids. The project was then constructed around two premises: it would be both a public space and a memorial. The memorial thus generates public space that becomes a model and medium for the city: a project that is open for the city and the people who claim it as their own.

The ruling concepts for the design are:

1. An open and active memorial: a living space in constant transformation that suggests peace, life, and appropriation and that also evokes memory, reflection, sorrow, and hope.

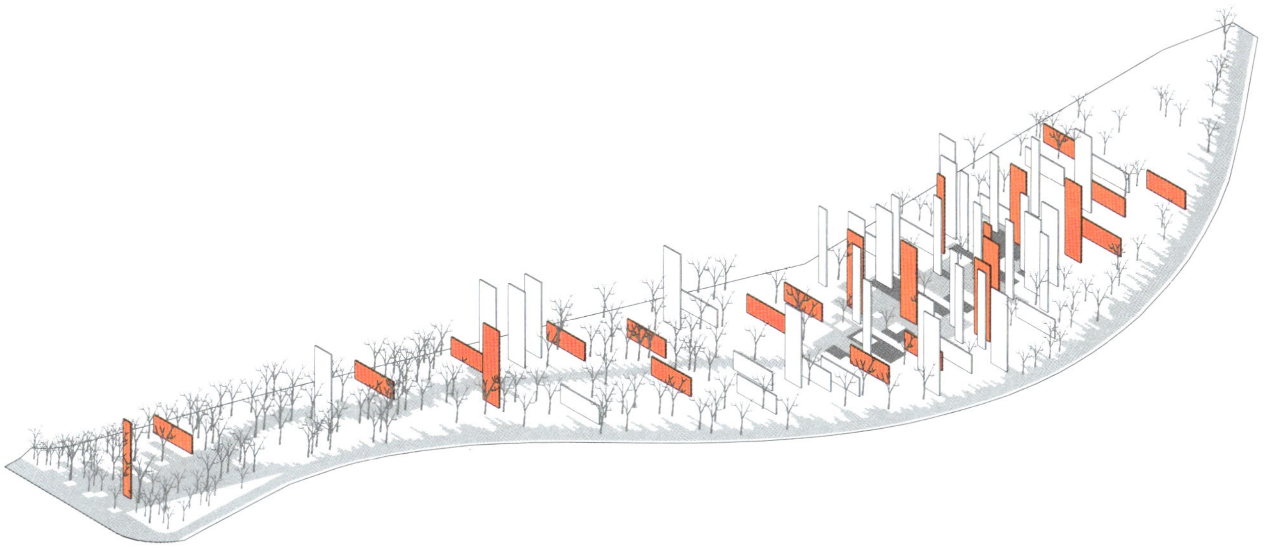

2. The invisible and the unfinished: this concept emerged as we wanted to build without occupying, to show voids and shadows, to create presence and denounce absences.

3. A forest of walls and trees: each wall penetrates the ground, almost slashing it, similar to how Lucio Fontana slits his canvas. The walls leave a minimum but deep mark from which the giants appear. Steel walls (that function as blackboards) emerge, generating voids between them and evoking the memory of those who have been lost.

4. Living materiality: a memorial that evokes peace should be expressed through its materials; it should represent death and also life and wear. That is why we used a minimal palette that only included steel and concrete. It is reminiscent of Richard Serra's sculpture materiality.

Designing, constructing, and implementing the project's concepts made us better architects and people. The memorial now stands as an urban banner and a reminder of peace, a dynamic place that keeps changing with the seasons in memory of those who are missing and with the presence of people who turn it into a place of solace, in a country where this is greatly needed.

LOCATION: Bosque de Chapultepec, Mexico City, Mexico / DATE: 2012 / SITE AREA: 15,000 sqm, 161,458.66 sf / DESIGN TEAM: Julio Gaeta, Luby Springall, architects / COLLABORATORS: Jesica Amescua, Jorge Torres, Brenda Ceja, Guillermo Ramírez, Edgar Martínez, Christian Ortega, Carlos Verón, Aldo Urban, Daniela Dávila, Miguel Márquez, José Luis Martínez, Juan Verón, architects / CONSULTANTS: Gustavo Avilés, lighting design; Hugo Sánchez, Tonatiuh Martínez, landscape design / CONSTRUCTION COMPANY, CONSTRUCTION MANAGEMENT: Federal Government of Mexico and Non-Governmental Organizations Against Violence in Mexico: SOS, Alto al Secuestro y Camino a Casa / TEXT: Gaeta Springall Arquitectos / PHOTOS: Sandra Pereznieto

When we saw the site, we knew its vocation had to be a forest; in more than one way, the pre-existing landscape suggested how the space had to be arranged. Landscape plays a fundamental role in the city and the memorial inserts itself as an urban piece that respects the site's pre-existing characteristics at the same time as it constructs public space that becomes a model and medium for the city. Therefore, our proposal envisioned a project that was left open to the forces of time, for the city and for the people.

—Gaeta Springall Arquitectos

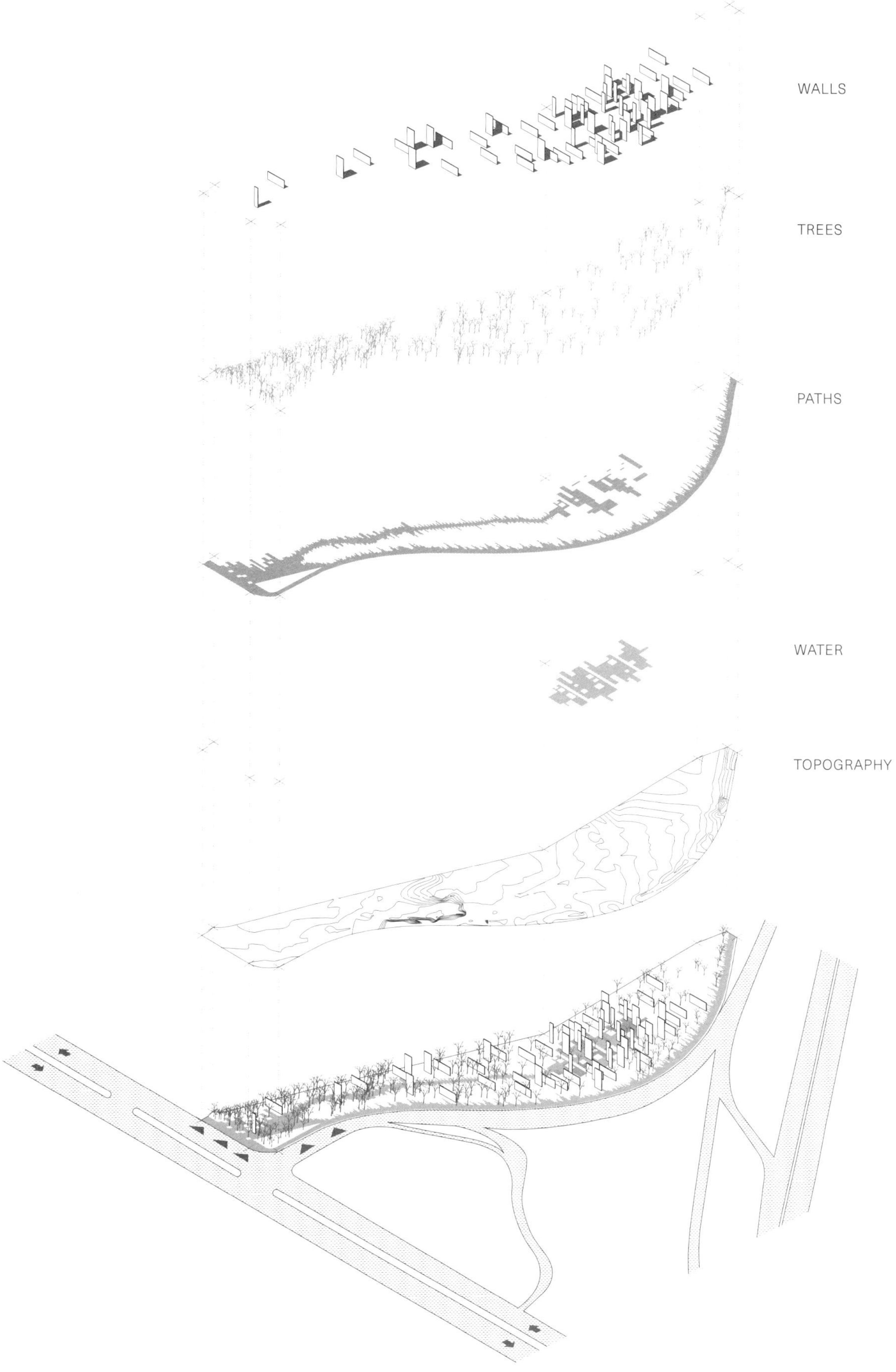

WALLS

TREES

PATHS

WATER

TOPOGRAPHY

EXPLODED AXONOMETRIC

Public space is rerouted through the curved shape of the glass. The reflecting surfaces dematerialize the boundaries between natural and artificial. Their combined effect creates a narrative for thinking about the place from which you are looking, creating a distinct and non-traditional situation in an urban park.

Your Reflection

CHILE

Guillermo Hevia García,

Nicolás Urzúa

Your Reflection is the result of a collaborative project between Guillermo Hevia García and Nicolás Urzúa, and this text refers to their positions on this project specifically, and landscape urbanism in general, rather than their individual practices.

"We believe we are a country and the truth is that we are just landscape." –Chilean antipoet Nicanor Parra.

This sentence has the power to question and unveil the main task of Chilean architecture. At the same time, it points directly to the fragility of a human relationship with landscape. Architecture has the power to work and make a real change in cities and landscapes. In Your Reflection, the creation of the natural (and yet artificial) landscape, both within the pavilion and the park, is what converts it into an architectural device, working as an experience-enhancer that can transport us and intensify our reflective experience.

When asked to measure a good city, one might list the possible activities and the access to quality spaces it offers its inhabitants. Activities and projects intended for leisure are a good scale for measurement. This pavilion is inserted into this logic—in the middle of a public space—offering its visitors an unconventional experience. We wanted to center the object's proposal on the experience of the subject. We did not intend to build a closed proposal but rather to articulate a universe of sensations and experiences that are open to many interpretations.

We understand that Latin American cities are not homogenous; they are a multiscale reality that changes from one country to the next. Problems of density or a lack of both civic and recreational public spaces—issues prevalent in cities around the world—are even more acute in the cities of the Southern Hemisphere. In cities that are constantly growing with extreme inequality, these basic conditions are magnified. In this context, landscape planning can be an effective tool for democratizing the city.

This situation represents the starting point for the construction of the landscape as an emerging practice in Latin America. In Chilean cities, a major challenge is

the inequality of the built environment; these conditions have led us to a violent social segregation that has turned into a political crisis. Another challenge is related to the role of the public realm. Chilean cities are a succession of privatized spaces, and we need to change the focus from the private dimension and turn it to the public arena. Two scales of intervention look to confront this inequality. The first seeks long term results, incorporating planning and landscape in the city's transversal development policies and attempting to understand landscape not only in terms of its large-scale surroundings but also as a series of conditions related to climate change. Sunlight or natural ventilation might be a starting point for the design. The second looks to short term change; this is where we believe our field of action is located. These interventions are small or medium in scale and deploy architecture and landscape projects throughout the city with the aim of renewing deteriorated or socially marginalized sectors.

The richness of Latin American's natural landscape must be transferred to our cities to transform them, to give them an identity and build spaces for interaction, a flexibility of use and a true public spirit.

LOCATION: Parque Araucano, Santiago, Chile / **PROJECT DATE:** 2015 / **CONSTRUCTION DATE:** 2016 / **SITE AREA:** 600 sqm, 6,458.35 sf / **DESIGN TEAM:** Guillermo Hevia García, Nicolás Urzúa, architects / **COLLABORATORS:** Felipe Droppelmann, Cristian Fuhrhop, Cristóbal Montalbetti, Diego Rivera / **CONSULTANTS:** Hunter Douglas Chile, structural engineering and construction
TEXT: Guillermo Hevia García and Nicolás Urzúa / **PHOTOS:** Adrian Aleson

EXPLODED AXONOMETRIC

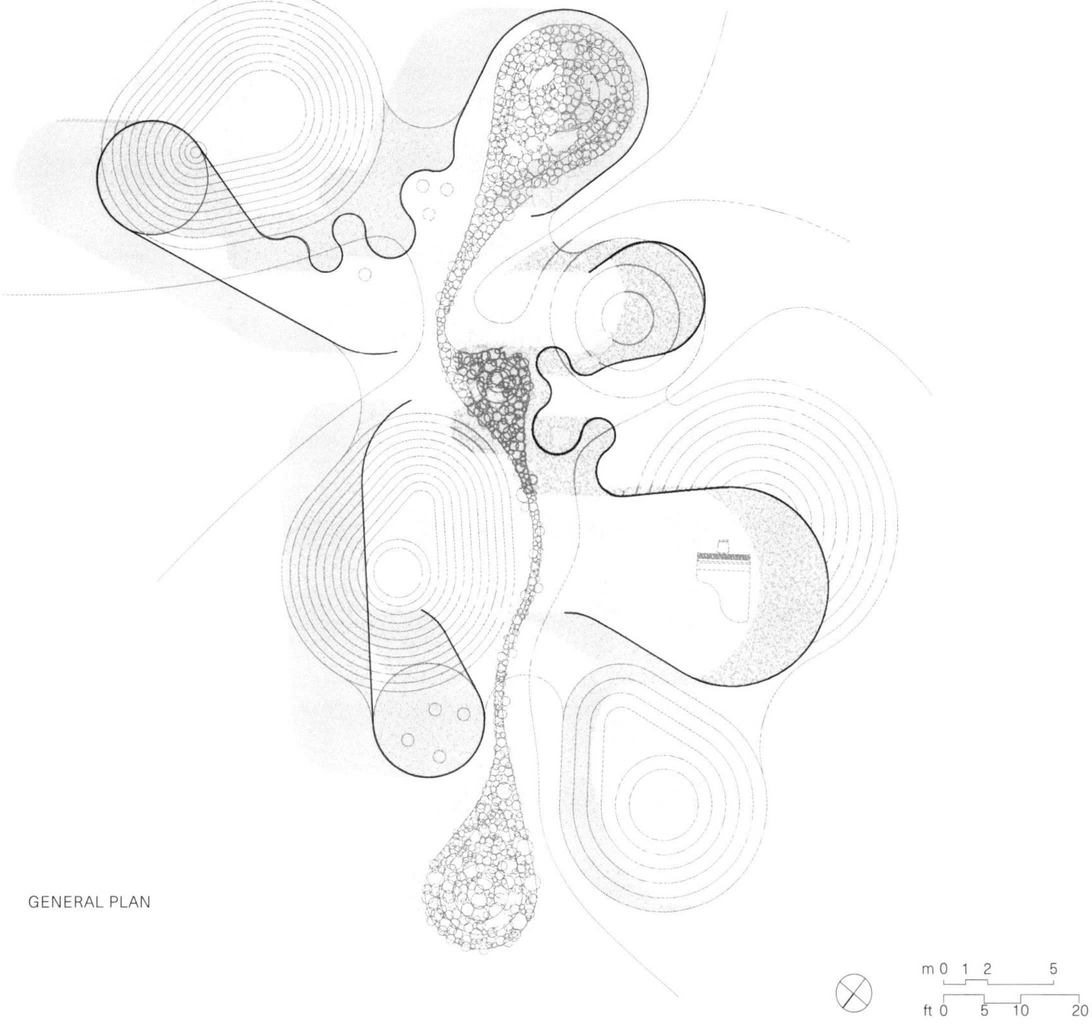

GENERAL PLAN

m 0 1 2 5
ft 0 5 10 20

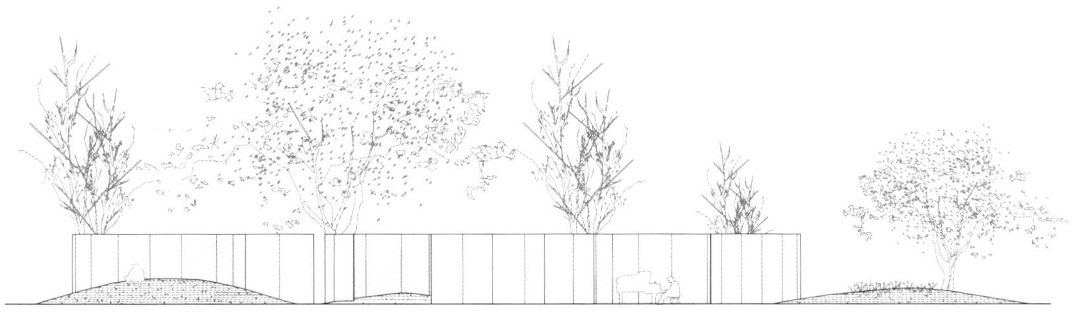

ELEVATION

Punta Pite is its own subtly designed world. The rugged coastline is domesticated but harmonized with its geological surroundings in a curated view that is open to the forces of the wild.

Punta Pite

CHILE

Teresa Moller Landscape Studio

The evolution of my work is related to every experience I have gathered in the development of the projects I have been in charge of, where I have found a deep understanding that we are part of the landscape; we are permanently related to it. Today it is well-known that our manner of approaching the relationship with our planet has been equivocal, especially these last forty years. I have been working on this subject for over thirty years and I have witnessed this lack of consciousness and its consequent deterioration. It is interesting to note that the reality that our planet is facing puts us on the spot, it makes the re-direction our design proposals towards sustainability urgent; it makes us seek that quality in each project.

Our practice has always been to inspire others, to invite people to experience nature. Our projects are designed on the bases of sustainability, economy, and design. What we look for is to find the essence of the site and work within what exists. I find my reference in each place I work.

LOCATION: Papudo, Quinta Región, Chile / DATE: 2005 / SITE AREA: 110,000 sqm, 1,184,030.15 sf / LANDSCAPE DESIGN: Teresa Moller, architect / COLLABORATORS: Francisca Aldunate, Camila Vicari, Catalina Legarreta, Francisca Piwonka, Catalina Philips SCULPTURE: Gerardo Aristía, Aymara Zégers / CLIENT: Condominio Punta Pite / PHOTOS: Chloe Humphreys

Landscape as Urbanism in the Americas in Review

Since 2016, the Landscape as Urbanism in the Americas conference series has convened a series of discussions on the potentials for landscape as a medium of urban intervention in the specific social, cultural, economic, and ecological contexts of Latin American cities.

March 15, 2016.
Museo de Arte Moderno de Medellín MAMM, Medellín

March 18, 2016.
Pontificia Universidad Católica de Chile, Santiago

March 21, 2016.
Espaço Israel Pinheiro, Brasilia

June 28, 2017.
Museo Tamayo, Mexico City

May 28, 2018.
Museo de Arte Latinoamericano de Buenos Aires MALBA, Buenos Aires

March 27-28, 2020.
Harvard University Graduate School of Design GSD, Cambridge

Participants

Sebastián Adamo & Marcelo Faiden. adamo-faiden, Buenos Aires

Miquel Adrià. Arquine, Mexico City

Israel Álvarez. Módulo 11, Mexico City

Tomás Alvim. Arq.Futuro, São Paulo

Marcos Amadeo, Frenando Cynowiec, Juan Granara, Adrián Russo & Alexis Schächter. Monoblock, Buenos Aires

Jorge Ambrosi. Ambrosi Etchegaray, Mexico City

Pedro Aparicio. Harvard GSD, Cambridge – Estudio Altiplano, Bogotá

Lucía Ardissone, Ana García Ricci & Ignacio Fleurquin. Bulla, Buenos Aires

Fabio Ayerra, Marcos Castaings, Martín Cobas, Federico Gastambide, Javier Lanza, Diego Pérez. Fábrica de Paisaje – Universidad de la République, Montevideo + Pablo Gerson. Universidad Torcuato di Tella, Buenos Aires

Mario Ballesteros. Andamio – Archivo, Mexico City

Brigitte Baptiste. Humboldt Institute, Bogotá

Anita Berrizbeitia. Harvard GSD, Cambridge

Tatiana Bilbao. Tatiana Bilbao Estudio, Mexico City

Alejandra Bosch. Pontificia Universidad Católica de Chile – LyonBosch+Martic, Santiago

Luis Eduardo Bresciani. Consejo Nacional de Desarrollo Urbano, Santiago

Melisa Brieva. Universidad de Buenos Aires, Buenos Aires

Pedro Camarena. LAAP, Mexico City

Loreta Castro. Universidad Nacional Autónoma de México – Taller Capital, Mexico City

Adriana Chávez. O-RU, Mexico City

Eduardo Chorén. Estancia Laguna Blanca, Entre Ríos

Colectivo Aqua Alta. Universidad Católica de Paraguay, Asunción

Eugenia Concha. El equipo Mazzanti, Bogotá

Pedro Henrique de Cristo. +D, Rio de Janeiro

Jean Pierre Crousse. Pontificia Universidad Católica del Perú – Barclay & Crousse, Lima

Serena Dambrosio. Universidad Adolfo Ibáñez, Santiago

Ana María Durán Calisto. University of California, Los Angeles – Pontificia Universidad Católica del Ecuador, Quito – Yale, New Haven

Luis Callejas. LCLA Office – Harvard GSD, Cambridge

Camilo Echavarría Gutiérrez. Universidad de Antioquia, Medellín

Alejandro Echeverri. Urbam, Universidad EAFIT, Medellín

Iñaki Echeverría. Echeverría, Mexico City

Gabriela Etchegaray. Ambrosi Etchegaray, Mexico City

Elisabete França. Studio2E Ideias Urbanas, FAAP – USP Cidades, São Paulo

Lukas Fúster. Universidad Nacional de Asunción, Asunción

Juan A. Gaitán. Museo Tamayo, Mexico City

Manuel Gausa. University of Genoa, Genoa

Agustina González Cid. Universidad Nacional de Rosario, Rosario

Andrew Harris. Harris + Illanes, Santiago

Romy Hecht. Pontificia Universidad Católica de Chile, Santiago

Sofía Heinonen. Tompkins Conservation, Buenos Aires

Alfredo Hidalgo. EAAD Tecnológico de Monterrey, Guadalajara

Martín Huberman. Monoambiente, Buenos Aires

Claudia Illanes. Harris + Illanes, Santiago

Helen Kongsgaard. Harvard GSD, Cambridge

Daniel Kozak. Universidad de Buenos Aires, Buenos Aires

Pablo Lazo. Arup, São Paulo

Arturo Lyon. Pontificia Universidad Católica de Chile – LyonBosch+Martic, Santiago

Claudio Magrini. Universidad Diego Portales, Santiago

João Manoel de Mello. Insper, São Paulo

Danilo Martic. LyonBosch+Martic, Santiago

Tonatiuh Martínez. Entorno, Mexico City

Juan Luis Mejía. Universidad EAFIT, Medellín

Felipe Mesa. Plan:B Arquitectos, Medellín

Cayetana Mercé. Clarín, Buenos Aires

Santiago Miret. Universidad Torcuato Di Tella, Buenos Aires

Sebastián Monsalve. Latitud, Medellín

Gabriel Díaz Montemayor. University of Texas, Austin

Roberto Montezuma. Universidade Federal de Pernambuco – INCITI – Parque Capibaribe, Recife

Rozana Montiel. Rozana Montiel Estudio de Arquitectura, Mexico City

Ciro Najle. Universidad Torcuato Di Tella, Buenos Aires

Catalina Patiño. CAPA, Medellín

Mercedes Peralta. Harvard GSD, Cambridge

Rodrigo Pérez de Arce. Pontificia Universidad Católica de Chile, Santiago

Pablo Pérez-Ramos. Harvard GSD, Cambridge

Sergio López Pineiro. Harvard GSD, Cambridge

Alessandra Ponte. Université de Montréal, Montreal

Juan Pablo Porta. Universidad Torcuato Di Tella, Buenos Aires

Francisco Quintana. Pontificia Universidad Católica de Chile, Santiago

José Alfredo Ramírez. Architectural Association – Groundlab, London

Emmanuel Ramírez. Estudio MMX, Mexico City

Marcela Ramos, Harvard University David Rockefeller Center for Latin American Studies, Cambridge

Camilo Restrepo. Urbam, Universidad EAFIT – AGENdA Agencia de Arquitectura, Medellín

Diego Ricalde. Estudio MMX, Mexico City

Víctor Rico. A-RU, Mexico City

Florencia Rodriguez. -NESS, Lots of Architecture -publishers

Luciana Sabóia. Universidade de Brasilia, Brasilia

Paulo Salles. Adasa, Brasilia

Hugo Sánchez. Entorno, Mexico City

Jeannette Sordi. Universidad Adolfo Ibáñez, Santiago

Belinda Tato. Ecosistema Urbano – Harvard GSD, Cambridge

Mariana Tello. Módulo 11, Mexico City

Elena Tudela. O-RU – Universidad Nacional Autónoma de México, Mexico City

Ana María Valderrama. Universidad Nacional de Rosario, Rosario

Duarte Vaz. EMBYÁ – Pontificia Universidad Católica de Río de Janeiro, Rio de Janeiro

Felipe Vera. Universidad Adolfo Ibáñez – IDB, Santiago

Paloma Vera. CanoVera Arquitectura – Universidad Iberoamericana, Mexico City

Fernando Viegas. Una Arquitetos – Escola da Cidade, São Paulo

Charles Waldheim. Harvard GSD, Cambridge

Diana Wiesner. Arquitectura y Paisaje EU – Fundación Cerros de Bogotá, Bogotá

Guilherme Wisnik. Universidade de São Paulo, São Paulo

Sponsors / Partner Institutions

Harvard University Graduate School of Design GSD

Harvard University Graduate School of Design – Office for Urbanization

Harvard University – David Rockefeller Center for Latin American Studies

Consejo Nacional de la Cultura y las Artes, Gobierno de Chile

Design Lab, Universidad Adolfo Ibáñez

Escuela de Arquitectura, Pontificia Universidad Católica de Chile

Universidad Católica Nuestra Señora de la Asunción

Facultad de Arquitectura, Diseño y Urbanismo UDELAR

Facultad de Arquitectura, Diseño y Arte, Universidad Nacional de Asunción

Universidad Nacional de Rosario

Escuela de Arquitectura y Estudios Urbanos, Universidad Torcuato di Tella

Facultad de Arquitectura Diseño y Urbanismo, Universidad de Buenos Aires

Urbam - EAFIT (Centro de Estudios Urbanos y Ambientales Universidad Medellín)

Facultad de Arquitectura Arte y Diseño, Universidad Diego Portales

Escola da Cidade, São Paulo

Facultad Arquitectura, Universidad Nacional Autónoma de México Escuela de Arquitectura, Arte y Diseño Tecnológico de Monterrey

Museo de Arte Moderno Medellín, Colombia

Espaço Israel Pinheiro

Museo Tamayo, Ciudad de México

Museo de Arte Latinoamericano de Buenos Aires MALBA, Buenos Aires

–NESS

PLOT

1:100

ArchDaily

Ladera Sur

Arquine

Inter-American Development Bank

LIGA Espacio Para Arquitectura DF

Empresa de Desarrollo Urbano, Medellín

Arq.Futuro

Adasa

Grupo Argos

Arup

Insper

Fundación Lemann

Buna

A conversation between

Last December, Boston, Buenos Aires, and Oslo virtually congregated to reflect on ideas developed in this issue and the Landscape as Urbanism initiative as a whole. Academic curricula, drawing as representation, constantly changing social and political spaces, the sensitivity around landscape, and other ideas were explored in the search for new paths of analysis.

Florencia Rodriguez
How did you decide to embark on this series of conferences in Latin America? I would like to start from there and then reflect on certain situations in that territory.

Charles Waldheim
It became clear to us, maybe five years ago or so that there seemed to be a set of changes that had occurred. These changes are diffuse, and of course there are enormous differences across different countries and cultures, but in the last five to ten years it became clear to me in my travels and conversations with people that something had begun to change.
Notwithstanding the value of that tradition or its persistence, for a number of reasons in the past couple of decades I've seen more architects from Latin America both studying and practicing abroad but becoming aware of—and bringing into their practices—a kind of biological thinking or ecological thinking or, in some cases, landscape. And then, similarly, I began to see evidence within Latin America, in different cultures and contexts, of architects who were choosing to identify as landscape architects and building new programs or chose to identify as landscape architects or ecological thinkers. And in that broad-brush kind of approach, I became aware, many, many years ago, of Luis's work and Paisajes Emergentes.

FR
Luis, how do you think this ecological and biological prompt started to grow, in your experience?

Luis Callejas
Well, first I will follow up with Charles. His observation is precise; however, my experience was slightly different. Most of the architects that had the chance to travel and get an education abroad before my generation went predominantly to Spain—perhaps a few to the Netherlands if they spoke some English, and very few to the United States. Colombia was in a crisis in the 90s, meaning that some of the best design talents had no choice other than getting experience or studying abroad. Thanks to that crisis, we had a few key talented practicing architects returning with masters and doctorates.
Some of them became instrumental in building relationships abroad and, more importantly, bringing a sensitivity towards the environment that was very present in Barcelona and Holland. Different sensitivities, for sure, yet both were key in updating the local way to relate to environmental issues. That moment coincided with the arrival of a new promising political class, surprisingly not skeptical of academia—in fact the opposite: politicians that invited some of these architects-academics to take an active part in defining future projects and even be part of the government.
Particularly interesting about Colombia is that those architects that helped formulate the known public landscape projects of the mid-2000s were not necessarily the ones designing them. Some of the most exciting projects were later done by a younger generation that didn't study abroad and had to react very fast to these exciting commissions—and certainly didn't have time to

Florencia Rodriguez

think about going abroad to pursue a second Master in Landscape Architecture. These were real commissions in the public realm that we got through competitions and that gave us the privilege to start our practices acting in the public realm.

When I graduated from Universidad Nacional in 2008, I had to decide quickly between studying landscape or doing landscapes. I decided to focus on practice. When I started Paisajes Emergentes, landscape urbanism was just beginning to resonate in Latin America; we saw it with distance and affinity at the same time, mostly via early blogs like the fantastic and short-lived "Pruned." At the same time, I had to start a practice with architects for an audience of architects, meaning that we had to define what landscape was to the even younger students and graduates that joined us in our small office.

To convince and motivate students to work for us, we developed a graphic language informed by landscape art, naturalists, botany, even landscape photography. I don't think it would be pretentious to say that we played a part in making landscape a promising as a possible path for other even younger architects in Colombia. However, it is important to admit that our dive into landscape happened too quickly—I always say that we were more like paramedics, that we had to react fast to commissions that came our way. [*Laughs*]

CW

From parametrics to paramedics. So you had a long tradition of Latin American architects studying abroad in Europe, specifically in Spain, following the flourishing of design culture in Catalonia in the 80s and 90s and then in the Netherlands in the 90s and 00s. You have a generation now that have gone abroad to these places and brought back a sensibility and have seen the role of landscape in those places, where, as you say, very large projects, very large infrastructural ambitions, are very much tied to political projects. And I think this has been a long durée tradition in Latin America—political leadership, especially mayors at the city scale, appointed or elected with the responsibility of delivering the public realm. But, in this case, we have coming back from Catalonia, coming back from Barcelona, coming back from the Netherlands, from Rotterdam and other places, the idea of these large infrastructural landscape projects.

But what's interesting in what you say is that it was practitioners who had been trained in the interior—in Colombia, in Chile, in Argentina—responding to those opportunities and connecting them to political programs. I think it is also interesting to mention here that in the course of the last several decades we see across the region a trend line generally moving towards forms of democracy—although of course there are questions around that everywhere these days—and a tendency of moving away from state dictatorships and military governments and toward open markets. We see much more trade; you can see evidence of that in the ease with which low-cost airlines have been connecting Latin America to itself. And, in a way, the interior political and economic condition is maturing.

I see this also reflected in the aspirations of the middle class in my travels in Latin America. The middle class seek to educate their kids, they seek to have a certain lifestyle, a certain quality of life, and in that case the idea of landscape amenity, the idea of remediating the brownfields, cleaning up the riverfronts—this, of course, corresponds to a kind of demand-side politically, for these kind of big public projects.

FR

Yes, it is interesting to elaborate more on that. These people are coming from different countries with such different political scenarios and the governments you were mentioning are sometimes unstable in a way, impacting the chance of any long-term planning—which is critical in any landscape project. Also, it is hard not to think now about what has been going on in Chile, in Bolivia, and in different parts of the region. How can the idea of landscape urbanism contribute to rethinking the city? Because a big part of the conflicts going on are related to the welfare state, and the things that it should ensure, the city being its main physical representation.

CW

Yeah, I think it is important to try and connect these things to the political and economic level, and they are very different of course in Western Europe, the examples in Spain and the Netherlands, and the kind of welfare state economies there, and very different than in North America, where we have essentially given up on the idea of public housing in favor of a neoliberal, Darwinist kind of culture. It's true that the political conditions are variable in different contexts, but broad-brushed there is the idea that there is an economy across the region of Latin America that is supporting the development of large, landscape-driven parks and projects, and that seems different than it would have been in a generation or two ago—the intellectual framework but also the practical capacities of the designer or architect.

LC

Correct, it is fair to say that some of these countries were and are politically unstable. However, remember that for us the end of that decade was in fact good, especially compared to previous decades where the was little hope for doing anything in the public realm. We felt like we were the first generation to have that privilege.

CW

So, Luis, the situation you are describing in the early or mid-2000s maps onto my experience from the outside. Can you say something more about to what extent you were aware of the things going on across the region? Did you sense that there was something comparable happening in bringing landscape ideas into other countries in the region?

LC

My generation was particularly interested in Brazilian modern design culture, their approach to the landscape as media, Mexico, and perhaps later also Chile. In general, tropical modernists were critical influences for us. We knew and admired Roberto Burle Marx, Costa, Barragán, but also looked at the work of Teodoro Fernández Larrañaga, Alberto Kalach, Sérgio Bernardes, Teresa Moller, and others. If the references from architecture and landscape were mostly modern, the references from art were avant-garde. Colombia has always been much more forward-thinking and global in the art world, particularly its relation to the sciences as compared to architecture.

As I said, some friends and colleagues came from Spain and they brought an idea of landscape that was interesting yet somehow not completely formed—it was insufficient to deal with the tropics. It is known that Iberian design culture has resisted landscape, and somehow keeps it subordinate to architecture. I remember wanting to resist that influence of Spain, wondering why all architects slightly older than me had to bring in Iberian references all the time; interesting, for sure, but also limited in describing what landscape as a media actually can do. When later we start to get in contact with people like you, Charles, that generated curiosity for our practice and invited us to teach abroad, we suddenly got an appetite for looking into what landscape as an idea is in North America. An idea that seemed fully formed, or at least mature as a discipline and profession. It showed us that landscape didn't have to be subordinate to architecture. That I already suspected, and was confirmed by my years at GSD. I do have to admit that as much as that contact with North American academia was influential, my way of reacting in projects through form is still more driven by those early tropical modernists and artists I knew from before.

CW

That corresponds to my experience with landscape urbanism in Western Europe and North America, which was very much led by practice. It did not really emerge as a theoretical construct until it had emerged in practice, and I think that history has been well described, but what you are describing in Colombia or in other parts of Latin America looks very much like what happened in other parts of the world, in which conditions and practice changed so quickly that the architect needed to respond and simultaneously have a kind of ecological or a green politics, a green position.

At the same time, they were dealing with very large sites in the wake of industry—large airport abandonments or large industrial ground fields, or the reconstruction of large infrastructural problems in wake of modernity, and so that idea that it was led by practice and that you were a generation of practice that saw that opportunity sits comfortably with the history in other parts of the world.

I would say what's different, what's unique about your experience is that there was a kind of economic and maybe societal opening, there was a kind of stability emerging after years of other kinds of challenges. And in that stability, the strong tradition of the architect being commissioned to look at the public realm then manifested itself in a demand or an interest in things that were much more ecologically informed.

I liked the way that you described what happened in your experience—that you had to very quickly respond to that as an opportunity. Can you say more about how your training or your cultural sensibility prepared you for that? Colombia is not a culture that has a landscape architecture tradition, in my experience. I could be wrong

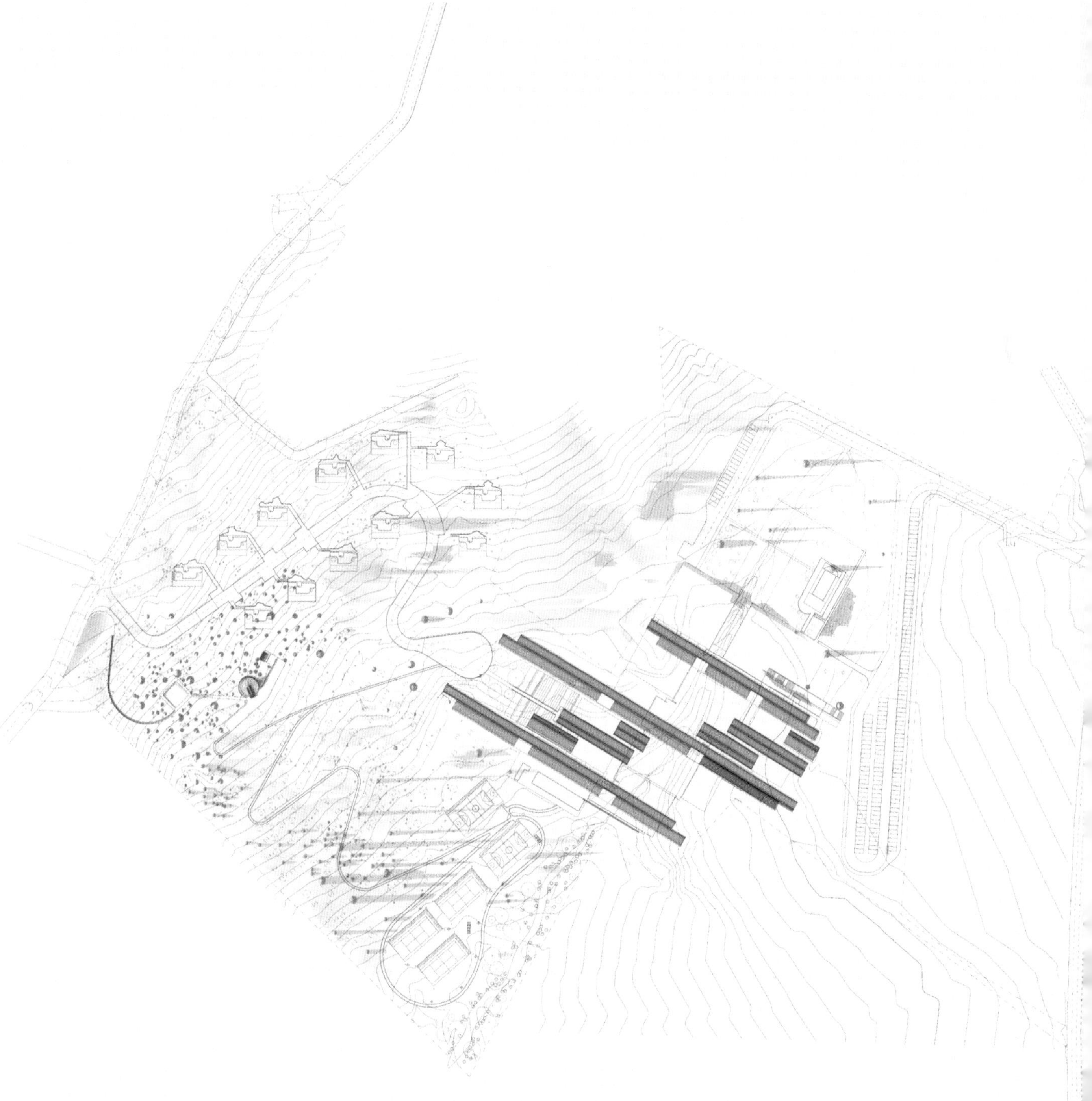

OBSERVATORY LANDSCAPE FOR ASTRONOMY COMPLEX AND HOTEL IN VILLA DE LEYVA, COLOMBIA, 2017
LCLA OFFICE (LUIS CALLEJAS AND CHARLOTTE HANSSON) AND EL EQUIPO MAZZANTI

IMAGE SHOWING THE STRUCTURE IN RELATION TO THE PALM COLLECTIONS IN THE TROPICARIO AT THE BOGOTÁ BOTANICAL GARDEN, 2013 / LCLA OFFICE (LUIS CALLEJAS AND CHARLOTTE HANSSON) AND EL EQUIPO MAZZANTI

about that, but I think it is one part of the world that has not really felt the need, historically, to develop landscape architecture as a unique discipline or profession, and so how does an architect working in Colombia respond to that as an opportunity?

LC
We had a fantastic architecture education that was closely linked to the natural sciences and geography. That was particular to the school I attended in Medellín, Universidad Nacional. That part of the university was actually called the "School of Mines" [*laughs*], which is essentially describing a part of the national university that trains professionals and engineers on how to read the territory and how to extract resources from it. Architecture in Medellín was born in that context, even the art school, meaning that understanding the complex Andean topography, vegetation, ecology, or even large infrastructural projects was part of the everyday of the school. We even had courses in tree architecture and basic botany, which by the way, was the most popular elective for architecture students. It's not like we suddenly dove into landscape without having any kind of education or background in its scales and media.

So there are places in which this might be something that becomes mainly operational, or pragmatic, and there is this other sensitivity toward this very omnipresent nature that makes it embedded in how you live and, consequently, how you are trained. Even though it doesn't always need the word "landscape" to be described. It's just part of the reality.

—Florencia Rodriguez

CW
In addition to the cultural reference, the geographical reference of the Andes, and the forest, you also have a history of an extraction economy, right, so the university being built around mining and extraction sites makes quite a lot of sense. But you also brought your sensibilities: your father is an artist, and you also brought a cultural sensibility to the idea of working with landscape as a medium beyond your professional training, no?

LC
It was also very important that both my father and mother were artists working with landscape. My father, Rodrigo Callejas, is a very recognized landscape artist, and my mother, Silvia Mujica, was an architect that quit architecture and did botanical illustration before developing her own body of work as an artist. My grandfather was a geographer and cartographer that wrote the geography books used in schools in Antioquia: he mapped the state while looking for mines as part of expeditions in the dense jungles.
There were many moments when that intense context of family and friends was much more interesting than the references coming from architecture. As my school was more like a polytechnic, there was a kind of intellectual void that was filled by this context of family, art, and landscape representation. We didn't have much theory in architecture school—that came from domestic life. However, we had excellent history courses: we had to draw the whole history of architecture over many semesters, and you know those drawings had backgrounds. The landscapes that I had to draw and were more interesting than some of the main subjects.

FR
While you were talking, in my head I was going through the singularities of Latin America in terms of topography and the exuberance of nature, which is very much conditioning how each country reacts or responds to the idea of landscape. So there are places in which this might be something that becomes mainly operational, or pragmatic, and there is this other sensitivity toward this very omnipresent nature that makes it embedded in how you live and, consequently, how you are trained. Even though it doesn't always need the word "landscape" to be described. It's just part of the reality.

CW
It's interesting—there's obviously a very strong and very variable botanical history, a very strong set of historical relationships to the non-human across the region and

various cultures and, at the same moment, there's been the idea that landscape was historically outside the city, somewhere on the horizon. And I think in that regard, one of most interesting and subtle and most problematic to translate is this issue of what Luis referred to as landscape becoming a medium of design: the idea that landscape does not exist out there on the horizon, it's not in the Andes, it's not in the forest or the jungle; in fact, it's a medium that we can control, it's plastic, it's a cultural form, it's relational.

And to the level of translation that you mentioned, Florencia, all the way through questions of representation to project formation, I think there's obviously still a lot of interesting and open questions. I'm quite convinced that the language that has developed in Western Europe and North America around these topics is probably inadequate to the conditions of Latin America and, out of this conversation, my goal for us is to begin to develop a kind of shared discourse about what terms of reference are most relevant. I'm very clear on the idea that simply importing an idea like landscape from Western Europe or North America is kind of problematic and not so interesting.

FR

When I think about the word and its translation I'm not only referring to that but I'm also wondering if you find some differences in the understanding of it in the same language—Spanish. What I feel is that when we talk about landscape or *paisaje* in different countries of the region we are referring to different things. So it's not a question of just importing or just a cross-relationship between two very different academies or orders (North and South), but more about the sensibility and tradition representing these Latin American countries. What happens in Argentina, where you see the majority of the big scale projects, is that they are done by the government. There are only traditional architects involved, that—very differently from what Luis was describing about Colombia—haven't been trained to think about landscape, or aren't even joining that conversation.

CW

This is an important distinction, I think. On the one hand, I think it is important to reference that landscape architecture as a new field in the 19th century emerges in a very specific cultural context to solve certain particular problems, and I think there's a limit to its generalization or its export, let's say. It's a field on its own that has quite a lot of growth just now in many parts of the world, but it's also a field that's maturing in Western Europe and in North America. I'm quite open-minded or maybe even ambivalent about whether landscape architecture would be relevant or not. I'm more interested in the conversation we were having earlier about the architect who's biologically or ecologically minded.

And the projects we've been looking at in Latin America over the past couple of decades range from large river remediation projects or large brownfield remediations all the way through a whole range of other kinds of things, which is really about an ecological sensibility or biological sensibility by the architect. And I think the plurality of that and the diversity of that is a strength, and I would recommend that going forward, much more so than simply the export of a new profession for its own sake.

LC

Yeah—on the one hand, I find extremely interesting that perhaps an affiliation to a discipline is not so important in Latin America. Architects have a particular sensitivity, some even plant literacy; on the other; there are more and more young architects that went to study abroad that are returning to Latin America with a landscape degree. I am speaking broadly about architects that are younger than me, perhaps were even influenced by the work that we do, and went out to pursue a second degree in landscape architecture.

Most of them went to North America, and those that returned are doing exciting projects or even starting new practices, they find themselves competing or collaborating with older architects that work with landscape through practice. I see that something promising is happening in these collaborations, and even in the intense competition that is starting to happen when these young designers return, especially the ones with a double degree. Double degrees are not so common in North America and Europe. As long as there are more interesting projects to do, and open access to them, I don't think it is an exaggeration to expect that Latin America can become a superpower for landscape practice. It could be due to the combination of highly-trained, double degree young designers plus the relevance and impact of public projects. The tropical context just adds interest.

CW

It's true that in our culture in North America there had been a kind of historical taboo against "both-and," at certain moments of time. It changes historically, of course, but I think that's one of the great changes in the past decade or two. It is now more and more common for architects to seek a second experience or second degree,

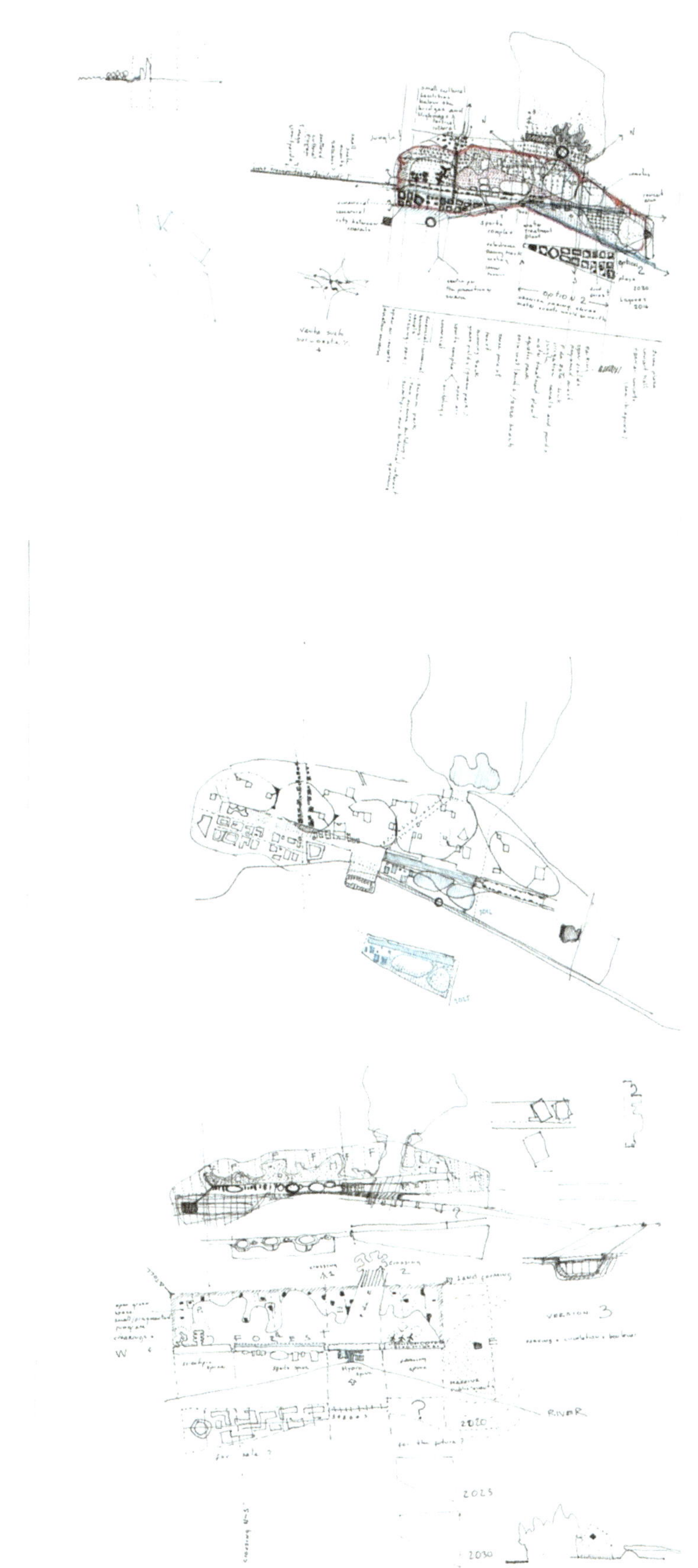

SKETCH FOR THE TRANSFORMATION OF LA CARLOTA AIRBASE TO AN URBAN PARK, 2012
LCLA OFFICE (LUIS CALLEJAS AND CHARLOTTE HANSSON) AND ANITA BERRIZBEITIA

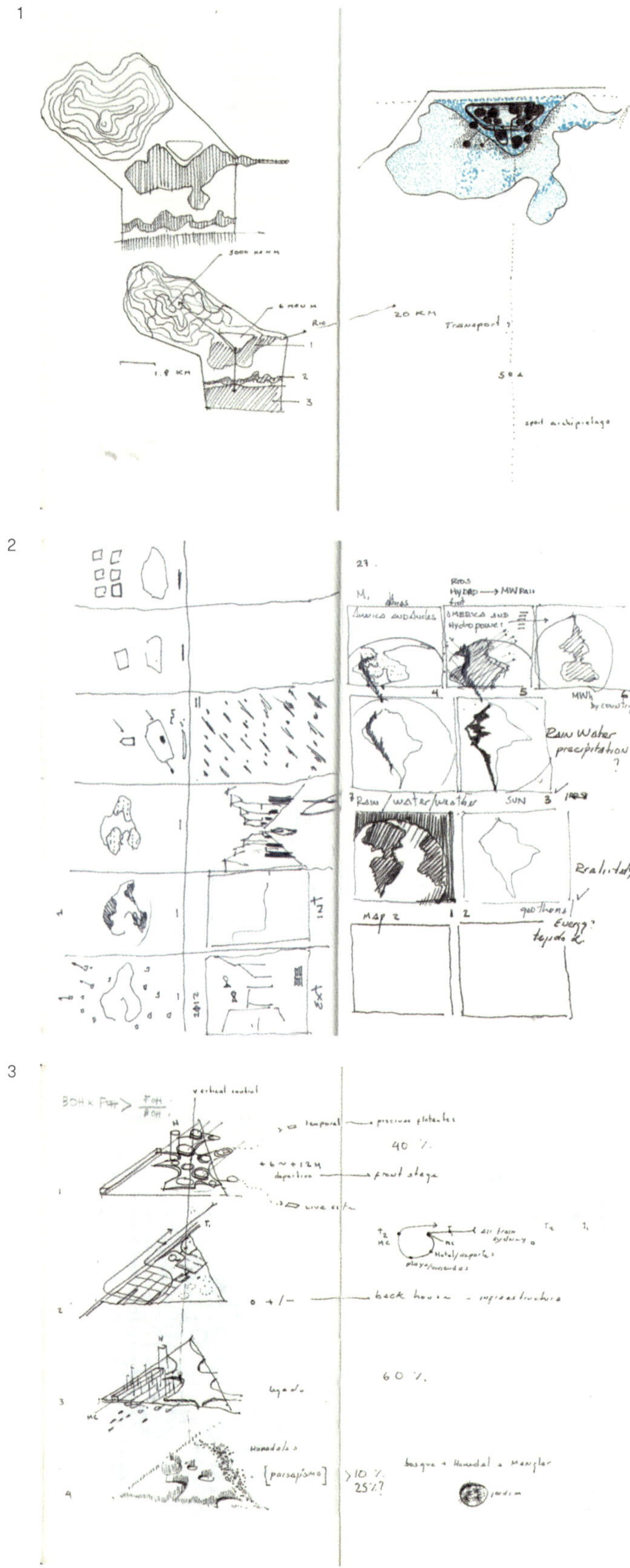

1. SKETCH OF THE MASTERPLAN FOR THE 2016 OLYMPIC GAMES IN RIO DE JANEIRO, 2010 / 2. SKETCH FOR HYDROBORDERS, 2011
3. SKETCH OF THE VERTICAL STACKING AND LANDSCAPE. MASTERPLAN FOR THE 2016 OLYMPIC GAMES IN RIO DE JANEIRO, 2010
LCLA OFFICE (LUIS CALLEJAS)

and I think that hybridity characterizes the plurality that we're describing. But when I step back from professional formation, when I look at work, what I see is a kind of evident sensibility. You can see a kind of landscape sensibility—whether it's about plan, material, or ecological thinking, or biopolitics, or whatever scale it is operating at, you can see and differentiate projects that have a kind of landscape sensibility to them.

If I were asked to describe what is Latin and particularly effective about this way of working with landscape, I would say that, generally, it is the capacity to translate environmental issues to defined form, and to work freely with abstraction, to find effective formal translations of the world of living things or natural sciences or geography. When translations are effective and distant from traditions we can see glimpses of truly original work.

—Luis Callejas

LC
Yeah, that sensitivity is not new. When you look at the most important or at least more sensitive modern architects in Latin America, many of them disproportionally had plant literacy: they knew about plants, they were interested in gardening. Some of them also had that interest from a young age, not as a kind of retiree's hobby. You cannot say the same for modern architects in other parts of the world. I have been tracking this for some time.

So, what is perhaps new is that many young architects are finally getting an education in landscape. It's becoming easier for them to connect with a tradition of modern architects that had plant literacy and genuine landscape sensitivity. Because when you say working with landscape as a medium of design, it's always a question, well, what does that really mean? Does it mean that you know about plants? Well, that's clearly not enough. It's also a unique way of drawing, a way of seeing the world, it's also a way of understanding the landscape through specific techniques of representation, that, as I have found, many modern landscape architects in Latin America had from before. A sensitivity and appetite for working with living things, whether it's in Brazil with architects like Sérgio Bernardes or Lina Bo Bardi, or even Paulo Mendes da Rocha, whom I have learned knows a lot about plants. In Colombia, obviously Rogelio Salmona. There are many more.

CW
I want to build on that a little bit and say that in North America, it was a similar experience where landscape urbanism emerged precisely as a critique of a kind of postmodern urban form or a kind of neo-conservative or neo-traditional urban form, and we made very explicit links back to a history of Modernity that had been, I think, under-scrutinized in which landscape played a role. You know, for me, recuperating Hilberseimer's work and looking back at landscape planning in the middle of the 20th century was central to that project, and so I'm happy to hear you say that you see something similar in the histories in Latin America.

FR
I think here is something very interesting to trace, because if there is something that characterizes Latin American modernism as unique it is the way in which it is profoundly connected to its context and territory. This tendency has been theoretically described by some as "Tropicalism." So these biological and ecological prompts that Charles was referring to at the beginning were very present in the reconfiguration of this new world. Even though they generated different scale and aesthetic outcomes, these ideas were present across the continent.

CW
I think that's true. So you have an impulse towards modernity globally, you have a local or a regional condition in Latin America, or variable conditions in different cultures, which are responding with respect to

the mediums. And I think the third element we have to add is that you have nation-state building. Building entire cities, in certain instances, as capitals; and in other instances, building entire university campuses, building new housing estates—the imperative of the nation-state constructing itself, and these big institutions being built through the hand of a strong architect. That's also quite important to that story.

LC

Specific to Brazil and Colombia is that the sensitivity towards landscape and the natural sciences emerged in a context where abstract art was dominant. There is no disconnection (or opposition) between abstraction and nature, or the capacity to abstract the messy stuff of the landscape into form. And it is really interesting to see how many young architects and young landscape architects from Latin America have a quite sophisticated capacity to translate the stuff of the landscape into precise forms. It is not about metaphors.

This is the most dominant part of the legacy of Latin American landscape architecture, or sensitivity, which is the capacity to effectively translate this stuff that resists being translated into design. I see that other design cultures have struggled much more with the translation of living things or the natural sciences or ecology into precise geometry. Perhaps an advantage of Latin America is that the dominant landscape traditions were weak when compared to the tropical storm that modernist abstract art was. Kinetic art and op art mattered more than the English garden.

CW

One of the things that this suggests for me, Luis, is that between scientific knowledge on the one hand and botanical plant knowledge on the other there seems to be less of a contradiction in Latin America or South America. Whereas in the North we've become quite alienated from each other. In landscape architecture today, there are many landscape architects who have deep, deep plant knowledge, but they will tend to prioritize the plant and a kind of palette of design over ecological knowledge or ecological thinking, whereas ecological sciences have also developed to a point where it's at such a level of abstraction that it is quite divorced from the botanical or kind of species-specific realm. And you are suggesting that in the world in which you were formed, and you believe that your colleagues were formed in, there's no distinction, there's no contradiction between a kind of scientific knowledge and plant material.

LC

Yeah, and also that the capacity to abstract is also the tool for making the translation between disciplines effective, because that translation is quite tricky, as we all know.

Just to be more direct, if I were asked to describe the Latin superpower for working with landscape, I would say that, generally, it is the capacity to translate environmental issues to defined form, and to work freely with abstraction, to find effective formal translations of the world of the living or natural sciences or geography. When translations are effective and distant from traditions like the French or the English, we can see glimpses of truly original work.

> One of the great strengths of the architect, as a cultural formation, is that the architect is capable of working with abstraction, working without a site, working through the prototypical or the infrastructural. I think merging the hybridity of those sensibilities again is one of the strengths of this conversation.
>
> —Charles Waldheim

CW

Your comments just now made me think of the work of Tatiana Bilbao or Iñaki Echeverría Gutiérrez in Mexico, or the many examples you referred to in Argentina and in Brazil. And in fact this represents one of the ways in which this conversation can help us in the North. One of the challenges for us in North America has been a kind of liberation of open-endedness. The idea that things could be more fluid and not so master-planned was a very fundamental and important breakthrough in the 90s and the 00s, and in some ways is continuing to be productive;

at the same time, it's very difficult in the context of any particular political or economic or cultural regime to execute projects that never arrive in a formal resolution. And I think in that sense, Luis, a part of what you are describing is a set of practices or discourses that could really benefit from a global audience.

LC

Well, I think that I can speak mostly about my own experience, which is what I see in Northern Europe. I am based in Oslo, where landscape architecture is still seen and taught as a kind of site-specific discipline. What I have been trying to do—and I think this has been successful—is to infuse the idea that through critical representation and description of certain geographies, it is possible to learn to design with some independence of context. To challenge site-specificity. Make the drawing or the model the context. A real model.

Obviously, it makes sense as I am working in a context that is very different than the tropics; it would be shooting myself in the foot to try to work there as a kind of local arctic expert, which I'm not. We always go to a site with an idea; site visits are becoming a late means of verification rather than an early revelation. In practice it is the same. For example, we are now doing our first project in Norway, the landscape around the former American embassy designed by Eero Saarinen. A privileged location and the building is clearly a jewel. What kind of landscape to do now that the fence is removed? We have been studying Saarinen's visit and obsessions with Mexico, his interest in how buildings touch the ground independent from context. He went to see pre-Hispanic temples with Jørn Utzon, who, by the way, also used what he learned in Mexico for the Sydney Opera House's plinth. We are working in Oslo with the American embassy, and are thinking about pre-Hispanic plinths.

CW

I want to build on this idea of landscape thinking that is not site-specific. I think it's one of the conditioning attributes of the way that landscape architecture developed in North America and in Western Europe that it tended to draw its value system, in the 19th century, from a kind of transcendentalist intellectual tradition in the United States. If you look at Olmsted, or in the formation of the profession here at Harvard, or if you look at other Western examples, there tends to be a pastoralism, a transcendentalist intellectual tradition. And oftentimes for the landscape architect in that tradition, the meaning is derived from the site as an almost personal divination: personal proximate relationship to the site becomes what is important. And one of the great strengths of the architect, as a cultural formation, is that the architect is capable of working with abstraction, working without a site, working through the prototypical or the infrastructural. I think merging the hybridity of those sensibilities again is one of the strengths of this conversation. Hopefully, it's one of the sensibilities that these Latin American experiences can bring to our understanding of these topics elsewhere.

LC

The techniques that were developed by practitioners and educators affiliated with landscape urbanism in the last decades have evolved. Drawings have become so refined that they almost inform more than the actual real sites. The evolution of the project of mapping that has happened in North America and Europe is reaching a limit. However, these techniques are suddenly very compatible with what I described as a kind of Latin American skill of abstracting. Something that doesn't necessarily require digital skills but also doesn't fight against them.

You are getting these two things together, which is the evolution of the project of representation happening within landscape urbanism, plus the unusual capacity of Latin American architects and landscape architects to actually work with abstraction.